# INTERPRETATION AND APPLICATION

THE PREACHER'S TOOLBOX

COMMUNICATING GOD'S WORD WITH POWER

# INTERPRETATION AND APPLICATION

JEFFREY ARTHURS
BRYAN CHAPELL
JOSHUA HARRIS
HADDON ROBINSON
KEN SMITH
JOHN BEUKEMA
DAVID JACKMAN
And more...

Craig Brian Larson, General Editor

HENDRICKSON PUBLISHERS

**Interpretation and Application**

Hendrickson Publishers Marketing, LLC
P. O. Box 3473
Peabody, Massachusetts 01961-3473

ISBN 978-1-59856-959-9



*Printed in the United States of America*

*First Hendrickson Edition Printing — August 2012*



**Library of Congress Cataloging-in-Publication Data**

Interpretation and application.
p. cm. — (The preacher's toolbox ; bk. 3)
ISBN 978-1-59856-959-9 (alk. paper)
1. Bible—Homiletical use. 2. Preaching. 3. Bible—Hermeneutics.
BS534.5.I56 2012
251—dc23
2012017816

# TABLE OF CONTENTS

# FOREWORD

*"Wisdom is supreme; therefore get wisdom.*
*Though it cost all you have, get understanding."*
*(Proverbs 4:7)*

That verse certainly applies to preaching. As editor of PreachingToday.com since 1999, I have listened to many sermons, and it is sobering to consider how many ways preaching can go wrong, from bad theology to bad interpretation of texts, from extremes on one side to extremes on the other, from being a people pleaser to being a people abuser, from confusing hearers to boring them. If there is any group of people in dire need of wisdom, it is preachers.

We find that wisdom in Scripture in large measure, of course. But while the Bible is our all-sufficient source book for what we preach, and for the theology of preaching and the character of the preacher, it is not a preaching manual. For much of what we need to know about preaching in our generation, in our geography, we need wisdom from one another.

We need the insights of those who have preached for fifty years, who have seen fads come and go, who have made mistakes themselves, and who can keep us from repeating them. We need the new perspective of young preachers who understand where the culture is going in ways that veteran preachers may not.

We need to hear from contemporary preachers who have read the wisdom of the church collected over hundreds of years on the subjects of preaching, pastoring, the care of the soul, theology, interpretation, sermon application, human nature, communication. We need to hear the wisdom of other "tribes" within the church, for each denomination or movement develops its own way of preaching, with its particular strengths and weaknesses.

In this book series, you will find a breadth of such wisdom. Since 1999 PreachingToday.com has published articles each month from outstanding practitioners on the essentials of preaching. This series of books with Hendrickson will draw from that bank vault of wisdom, bringing you timeless wisdom for contemporary preaching with the goal of equipping you for the most important work in the world, the proclamation of the glorious gospel of our Lord Jesus Christ.

And week by week, through the ups and downs, ins and outs of their lives, your congregation will be glad they have come to the house of the Lord to hear you preach. In your voice, your flock will hear the voice of the chief Shepherd, the Overseer of their souls.

Let it be, O Lord, by your grace!

—Craig Brian Larson, editor of PreachingToday.com

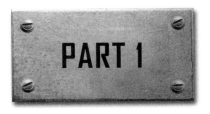

# PART 1

# Biblical Interpretation

# AS ONE APPROVED

*How to pass the preacher's test.*

*Douglas Sean O'Donnell*

I used to cheat in Algebra. Math has always been difficult for me. So when I was assigned to the honors algebra class, which was way over my head, I adjusted this discrepancy by "borrowing" some answers from the best mathematician in the school, a fellow starter on the varsity basketball team.

Though I wasn't a Christian at the time, I had a strong conscience, one that initially burned within me each time I broke the school's law, God's law, and my own moral law. But after a while, as the teacher himself turned a blind eye to what was going on, and my heart hardened toward this sin, this fire of conscience cooled. The guilt subsided. The teacher didn't care. My friend didn't care. I didn't care. I passed the class.

When I became a Christian a year after graduating high school, everything changed on the inside, and eventually on the outside. So when I transferred to Wheaton College to major in Bible/theology, I vowed never again to cheat on anything.

This vow, however, was quickly tested. In my second semester of New Testament Greek (which, I'm convinced, uses the same mental muscle as math), I missed the midterm exam due to the flu. My professor graciously allowed me to take the test on my own time. He told me he would leave a copy of it in his mailbox outside of his office. I could pick it up and take it whenever I felt better.

A few days later, in good health, I stood before his mailbox. I saw the test and grabbed it. Yet, as I looked down in the mailbox again, I noticed another exam, one completed by the best student in the class. I looked around. The hallway was empty. I cautiously lifted the other exam. It felt as heavy as a thousand fat devils dancing on it. Yet as heavy as it felt, it was as if a calm, reasonable voice whispered from it, "Take and copy. Take and copy." I heeded that advice. I placed both exams in my backpack and hurried across the street to the library. I zipped open the backpack, placed the blank test on the right, and then I lifted slowly the other exam.

Then . . . I stopped. I didn't place it down on the left. Instead, convicted by the Spirit—that God sees all, that cheating is a sin, that such a sin would be offensive to God, my teacher, and my classmate—I placed the completed exam in my backpack again. I walked back across the street, and I placed it back in the professor's mailbox. I returned to the library and took the test on my own. I passed *the* test! What a victory for me, one among many. For by God's grace I never cheated in college, graduate school, or seminary.

Now as a pastor, however, every week I'm tempted to cheat in other ways—not on a Greek test but on God's Greek text. More plainly, I'm tempted to disregard either the Bible (the Greek, Hebrew, or Aramaic text, thankfully translated into my own tongue) or principles of rightly interpreting God's Word. Or both! I'm tempted, as all pastors are, to bypass the Bible and biblical exegesis in an effort to wow the congregation with anything and everything but the Bible.

Here I want to challenge you to prepare sermons based on the conviction that no sermon is God glorifying if it ignores or mishandles God's Word. I will do so by briefly walking through four temptations we preachers face on a weekly basis. For each temptation I will offer a truth that we can use to uphold us when enticed to leave aside and/or compromise our fundamental convictions and practices of sound Bible preaching. I will conclude with a summary word from that rightfully famous preacher's text, 2 Timothy 2:15.

> *No sermon is God glorifying if it ignores or mishandles God's Word.*

## The first temptation

Our first temptation is to preach something other than the Bible as the source and essential substance of our sermon. These days the biggest evangelical churches have often embraced church-growth models. Such models often include (indeed part of the success is) sermons based less on Bible texts than on cultural topics. Having been raised as a Roman Catholic, where the Bible was rarely preached but often read in church, I find it quite ironic that these days you would likely hear more Bible on a Sunday morning in the Catholic liturgy than from a Protestant pulpit. We must protest such new Protestantism and resist its lure.

The conviction to ward off this temptation says, when the Bible is preached God's voice is heard. When I lead a workshop on biblical exposition for the Charles Simeon Trust, my first lesson usually begins by answering the question, why does expository preaching matter?[1] At my most recent workshop in Dublin, Ohio, I included some quotes from two authors that nicely solidified my thoughts (and personally reconvicted me!).

The first author is John Owen. In his classic *Of the Mortification of Sin in Believers* (first published in 1656), he writes (and I paraphrase):

> Sometimes as we read the Word, God makes us stay on something that cuts us to the heart and shakes us as to our present condition. More frequently it is as we hear the Word preached that God meets with us, for preaching is God's great ordinance for conviction, conversion, and edification. God often cuts us by the sword of his Word in that ordinance, strikes directly on our bosom-beloved lust, startles the sinner, and makes us engage in the mortification and relinquishment of the evil of our hearts.

Is that your conviction? Do you think "sacramentally" about preaching—that it is God's "great ordinance" for conviction, conversion, and edification?

The other author I quoted was Frederick Dale Bruner. In his lecture "The Shy Member of the Trinity: Expository Preaching Gives the Filling of the Holy Spirit," Bruner adds some fire to his usual light. Let the two quotes below burn within:

> Preaching and teaching that is born of a prayerful wrestling with the biblical texts in an almost athletic attempt each week to find the *real* meaning of these authoritative scriptural sentences—*that* is evangelical-catholic preaching and teaching. Such preaching and teaching is, when it pleases

> God to honor it, filled with the Spirit. . . . If believing Christ is the way we ourselves are filled with the Spirit . . . then interpreting Scripture is usually the main way that pastors are means of grace to the greater part of their people each week.[2]
>
> I love exegesis. But exegesis may not be every pastor's or teacher's main gift (1 Corinthians 12). Am I wrong, however, in believing that exegesis is almost every preacher's, and many church teachers', main *responsibility*?[3]

Bruner is not wrong. It is our main responsibility to join the nearly thirty centuries of Bible expositors before us to cohabit with the divinely inspired texts Monday through Saturday in order to speak on Sunday "the honest truth about the words of God to the real needs of the people of God,"[4] believing that "the Sunday morning sermon has been the ordinary conduit of the life-giving Spirit to the people of God through the ages"[5] and that God's voice is heard when his Word is opened, explained, and applied.

## The second temptation

Our second temptation is sermon-prep procrastination. We live in an age of remarkable advances in technology. Let's use that technology. We shepherd people who have real physical, emotional, and spiritual needs. Let's love people. However, let's not allow technology and people to persistently push us away from our study of Scripture. Sermon preparation is sacred time. It is as sacred as prayer, burying the dead, baptizing your first-born, and kissing your wife with Song of Solomon kisses.

Sadly, I know too few pastors who are in the habit of getting to this sacred duty and delight early in the week and often throughout the week. Rather than redeeming the time,[6] too many pastors (you?) cheat on getting to the text and then spending much time in the text because they fall prey to the temptation to reply to e-mails immediately, read twenty-four blogs every twenty-four hours (or is it twenty-four minutes?), chat on the cell phone, watch the must-see YouTube videos,[7] and refuse to say no to any unexpected office visitor. At their ordination these same pastors were likely commissioned to make their life verse "Preach the Word," but their weekly, out-of-context, much-perverted proof-text for procrastination has become "Do not be anxious beforehand what you are to say, but say whatever is given you in that hour, for it is not you who speak, but the Holy Spirit" (Mark 31:11 ESV). The foolishness of preaching and the foolish preacher are vastly different realities. And the pastor who thinks the Spirit will bless his sermon if he refuses to sit, read, study, and pray through that Spirit-filled book is foolish!

For this second temptation, the corrective measure is discipline. I don't mean a slap on the hand or the bottom (although perhaps starting there might get your attention). I mean learning the discipline of Spirit-filled *sitzfleisch*. *Sitzfleisch* is a German word composed of the words *sitzen* (to sit) and *fleisch* (flesh). I first heard this word from my church history professor in seminary. If I recall correctly, it was a term used often by the great Reformation scholar Heiko Oberman, referring to what it takes to be a good scholar. It takes "sitting flesh," that is, the ability to stay glued to a chair until the task at hand is complete. The same is true of the good preacher. The preacher who can't sit early and often meditating on Sunday's text will not preach well. I'll put it that simply and, Lord willing, prophetically. Let him who has ears, hear.

We are used to hearing the phrase *Spirit-filled preaching*, which emphasizes the Spirit spontaneously assisting the preacher in the act of preaching. I take no issue with Spirit-filled preaching so long as it is properly defined and acted out. Let us "give room" for the Spirit in the pulpit. But let us also "give room" for the Spirit in the study. Why not ask the Spirit to give you the desire to sit and study? Why not ask the Spirit to open your eyes to see the text's truths, implications, and applications? Why not ask the Spirit to inspire you to study the text in community—with other pastors, interns, commentators? Why not ask the Spirit to broaden your mind with the reading of the best books of poetry, novels, and theology? Why not ask the Spirit to make you a pastor-scholar, someone who lives and works by the discipline of Spirit-filled *sitzfleisch*?

## The third temptation

Our third temptation is to forget or neglect basic hermeneutical principles. You may not be able to spell hermeneutics (I misspell it every other time I type it), but you had better know basic hermeneutics.[8] To make the point more pointedly, I will simply list *ten* regular hermeneutical/homiletical questions that should be in your mind when your Bible is open before your eyes. These are all based on the theological assumptions that the Bible is a divinely inspired, accommodated-to-humans, and progressively written revelation.

1. Did you take at least half a day to make your own observations on the text?

2. Did you find the skeletal structure of the text?

3. Did you seek to understand how the original audience understood God's Word to them before you applied it to your hearers?

4. Did you interpret Scripture with Scripture ("the analogy of faith"), the unclear by the clear, and the implicit by the explicit?

5. Did you examine the text's context—its immediate context, the book's context, historical context (when and by whom it was written, if known), and literary context (genre)?

6. Did you examine the text in light of the main message of the book?[9]

7. Did you examine the text in light of the main message of the Book? That is, did you relate the text to the centerpiece of the canon—the person and work of Christ?

8. Did you, without straying from historical Christian orthodoxy ("the rule of faith"), allow the text to shape and change, if needed, your theological framework?

9. Did you read solid commentaries to help with difficult issues, correct your interpretation, and add exegetical insights?[10]

10. Did your applications come from what is explicitly or implicitly found in the text, or did you add your own legalisms or liberalisms to the Bible?

If I were to add an eleventh question, it would be related to the first; did you take at least the other half of the day to make more observations on the text? I emphasize the art of observation, and I'll end here with its emphasis, because I believe that good preaching is derived from pleasurable yet painstaking examination of God's Word. What the prominent New Testament scholar Adolf Schlatter said of the science of scholarship—that it is "first observation, second observation, third observation,"[11] I say of preaching. Sit. Read. Sit. Pray. Sit. Think. Sit. Write. Sit. Edit. Sit. Kneel. Sit. Stand. Preach.

## The fourth temptation

Our fourth temptation is to cower under cultural pressures. I have a pastor friend who the three Sundays before he left one church for another preached a series titled something like The Three Things I Always Wanted to Say to You, but I Was Too Afraid to Say. We might chuckle at that, but we all know that the twin pressures not to offend and easily to appease are no laughing matter. We all know the countercultural contents of our Bibles—those texts on Christ's exclusivity, Christian cross-bearing, the sinfulness of our sin, and the justice of God's judgment. It takes courage to preach the whole truth and nothing but the truth.

Last year my three-year-old church plant merged with an established church (technically the oldest in the county). The established church generously gave us their land and building and invited me to lead the united congregations as the senior pastor. What an honor. What a generous blessing! However, after I preached some initial sermons on the vision of the church, all based on texts from Luke's Gospel (don't worry—I didn't succumb to the first temptation and preach topical sermons on How to Make Our Church the Biggest in the State in Six Sure Steps), I was met with the temptation to stop preaching through the Gospel of Matthew. For, you see, the next text on the pre-merger preaching schedule was Matthew 23. Yikes. "Should I preach on Jesus' seven woes to this newly united congregation? How well will that go over? Will people think poorly of me, Jesus, or the both of us together?"

I have a conviction about preaching in sequential exposition through books of the Bible, which I'm committed to, and for me to break from this pattern at this point would have been a compromise for me. Trusting that those hard words from Jesus to the scribes and Pharisees were indeed God's word to his church today in some way (in more ways than I at first imagined), I walked us through the woes. Moving on in Matthew, we came next to that hermeneutical mountain we call the Olivet Discourse (Matt. 24–25). Together we journeyed through the destruction of Jerusalem and the end of the world as we know it, and there were no casualties. Rather, by means of his Word preached, God graciously matured us in ways we never could have imagined. That's the beauty of God's Word! Sometimes the hard texts (Matt. 23) are used to soften hard hearts, and the most complex ones (Matt. 24–25) are used to teach the simplest truths of the gospel.

The temptation to cower under cultural pressures can be met by our assurance that expository Bible preaching is right, real, and relevant. Like Moses on Mount Sinai, we are called to herald the Lord's decrees; like Ezra at the Water Gate, we are to read and help the people to understand the Book; and like Jesus in the Nazareth synagogue, we are to open the Scriptures and preach Christ. Expository Bible preaching is the right thing to do.

It is also the most authentic message to give. In a culture that is appealing for authenticity, the Bible proves itself to be real because it meets our real needs. What is our greater need: Physical healing or the forgiveness of sins (Matt. 9:2)? Food and clothing and shelter or seeking first the kingdom of God (6:33)? Bread to eat or the Word of God to know and obey (4:4)? Only the Bible provides the right answers.

Finally, the Bible is relevant. Themes in the Sermon on the Mount or the double-love command of Matthew 22:34–40 are obviously relevant. The beautiful thing, however, is how every inspired text ("all Scripture") is "profitable for teaching, for reproof, for correction, and for training in righteousness" (2 Tim. 3:16 ESV). Put differently, every part of the Bible is relevant. How true I have found this truth to be! Matthew's Gospel, for example, starts with a seemingly irrelevant Jewish genealogy. Yet study it, dive into it, see it for what it is, and the powerful themes of God's plan, providence, and timing emerge, and the glorious theme of Jesus as Savior of sinners, Gentile sinners, Gentile women sinners, sparkles like a thousand ten-carat diamonds in a deep but clear stream.

## A final word from the Word: 2 Timothy 2:15

In 2 Timothy 2:15, the apostle Paul enjoins Timothy to "Do your best to present yourself to God as one approved, a worker who has no need to be ashamed, rightly handling the word of truth" (ESV). This verse serves well to highlight the four convictions discussed above. Instead of preaching something other than the Bible, we are to preach "the word of truth"—the truth, the whole truth, and nothing but the truth. Instead of being time-wasting sloths, we are called to be "workers," working hard throughout the week. Instead of forgetting or neglecting basic hermeneutical principles, we are to "rightly handle" God's Word.

Instead of falling prey to the pressure of popularity, we give it straight, because we will stand before God "as one approved" or disapproved.

**Douglas Sean O'Donnell** is senior pastor at New Covenant Church in Naperville, Illinois, and author of *The Beginning and End of Wisdom* (Crossway).

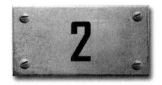

# 2

# LET THE TEXT QUESTION YOUR FRAMEWORK

*Learn to preach this text, in its context, for all its worth.*

*David Jackman*

Framework is both important and inevitable. It's important that our framework be as biblical as it possibly can be, and it's inevitable that there will be a framework. We would love to think that we could come to the Bible text as to a blank sheet, that we came with our minds completely open and there were no impressions in our mind. But of course that's totally impossible. And the longer we've been Christians and the more we've been serving the Lord, the more our framework is developed. That's not a bad thing. It's simply to recognize that it exists.

Suppose that I draw a small box that represents the text we're going to work on. As we come to study a passage for the purposes of expository preaching, how does the framework connect to the text? The most common thing—and this happens almost automatically without our recognizing it—is that the framework will pour its ideas into the text. It's a little bit like wearing a pair of spectacles as I come to the text. If I've got a pair of spectacles on, everything I see I see through the spectacles. My framework is my spectacles. I've got them on. So everything I see in the text I see through my spectacles. Inevitable. There'll be spectacles of twenty-first-century people who live in the West who've had the traditions that we've had, who've had the upbringing and the instruction that we've had. The framework will be different for all of us, but you can't escape it.

Now the question is, how do I stop the framework dictating my understanding of the text? Parts of the framework will help me, because the framework will have principles of exposition and exegesis and skills that I've learned. And all of that is good within the framework.

But the great danger is that I don't let the text speak for itself. Sometimes I express it like this: the congregation can always tell when you've had a hard week, because you will preach your framework rather than the text. You know how it happens: There are two or three emergencies; there are extra things like funerals you haven't scheduled. You get to Saturday, and you haven't done the work on the text you wanted to.

*The congregation can always tell when you've had a hard week, because you will preach your framework rather than the text.*

Well, the great blessing is that there are things in the text that trigger ideas in the framework. So isn't it a mercy that the text has grace in it? Because grace is a great framework theme. "There's the illustration, and there's the cross-reference that I found last month, and there's what I've said before. . . ." It might be called GRACE: **G**od's **R**iches **A**t **C**hrist's **E**xpense. And all of these things are triggered from the framework. Isn't it a blessing—that here on Saturday night, I can pour the framework into the text?

God is very gracious and very good and often uses that—at least in my theology on the basis of it being an emergency. But it is not a philosophy on which to build an expository ministry. We all have experiences of God being good to us in helping us through difficult times when we've been up against it because of pressures. But normally we don't want to be simply pouring the framework into the text.

We want the text to be impacting the framework. The text asks all sorts of questions about the framework. And that is what I mean when I talk about coming to the text with our antennae up, trying to hear God, being careful listeners, not cool analysts. The cool analyst will say, "I've got the framework for this. I've got the grid. It's this bit of my systematic theology. *Plunk*. There it is on the text. That is what is going to dictate the sermon."

That is preaching that may be theologically accurate, and it may be perfectly orthodox, but it's not preaching *this* text in its context for all its worth. And biblical exposition lets the Bible do the talking. The framework will inform—you can't be without it—but keep asking the questions. One of the keys to interesting preaching is the surprises that the preacher finds. If you're not being surprised by the text, don't expect that there will be any eye-opening moment in the congregation. We don't have to manufacture surprises. If we read it carefully, there always will be fresh things that come up.

We then have to sort out whether they're important or not. Sometimes I'm surprised by what seems at the end to be insignificant detail. You don't build a sermon on insignificant details. You've always got to go for the main thing the passage is teaching. And sometimes you can have so many surprises that the congregation would be in a state of permanent shock if you put them all into the sermon. You've obviously got to feed them and teach them the content of the passage, the meat of the Word, the real thrust of this particular passage. But I think it is true to say that, as I keep on trying to preach—and I've been doing it now for thirty-five years—I am constantly surprised by the way in which the Bible speaks to me—and you—fresh.

When you get down to the work, the text asks all sorts of questions. Your framework develops. You may have an extension built on here, because you never understood that before. Or maybe you've crossed out here, because your framework has changed; if your framework is the same now as when you came out of seminary, that's a really, really sad situation. I'm not trying to turn you into a heterodox person or heretic, but I do mean that we ought to be growing in our understanding and appreciation. Don't get set in your ways so that you're just stuck in concrete. *Do* let the text constantly challenge your thinking so that your thinking becomes more biblical. I think that's what the founding fathers meant when they talked about more light and truth to break forth from God's holy Word: we're understanding it better, and we're growing in our knowledge of God and in our love for him.

So text and framework is an important discipline. And there's a danger in simply pouring the framework into the text. Let the text question the framework. Then you'll always be learning new things. Then your congregation will also be learning with you.

It's a mark of a man like Dick Lucas with whom I've worked for a number of years. When he came as a guest preacher when I was a young pastor in South Hampton—this would be twenty-five years ago—he said to me, "Oh, brother, do pray for me. I've got this all completely wrong." Which was an enormous encouragement to me because I often feel like that. Don't you when you go into the pulpit?

Of course he preached the most wonderful sermon; he hadn't got it completely wrong. I think what he meant was that he's always asking questions. He's always searching. "Have I got this really right?" It's that sort of inquiring mind that is so important and so significant for an effective expository ministry.

**David Jackman** served as president of the Proclamation Trust and is the founder of the Cornhill Training Course. He is a visiting lecturer at Oak Hill Theological College in London and author of *Opening Up the Bible* (Scripture Union Publishing).

# 3

# PREACHING THE MELODIC LINE

*How the grand themes enrich a sermon.*

*Dick Lucas*

*This interview with Dick Lucas, longtime pastor in Bishopsgate, England, and a champion of expository preaching, focuses on how our understanding of the running ideas of a biblical book enhances everything in a sermon.*

**What do you mean when you talk about preaching the melodic line of a text?**

I didn't invent the term *melodic line,* but it has become quite well known. The melodic line is taken from the fact that a piece of music has a tune or a line going through it that holds the whole thing together. We want to show that in a New Testament letter, for example, a theme holds the whole thing together. Therefore, to take verses and passages out of the context of that melodic line, that theme, that argument that runs through the letter, would not be profitable.

For example, 2 Timothy 3:16 is often pulled out to prove the inspiration of Scripture, which, of course, it does prove. But if you put it in the melodic line of the letter, you find it is Paul's instructions to Timothy as to how he is to continue his ministry, and Paul is saying the one equipment Timothy needs for his ministry is the Word of God, which will enable him and train him in righteousness and correction and all the rest of it. I know a principal of a theological college who is determined to bring everything in the curriculum under 2 Timothy 3:16. That is, he wants the Bible to control all the other disciplines. That's really what Paul is saying to Timothy. Although the verse does teach the inspiration of Scripture, and indeed without inspiration the Scriptures would not be powerful to do the work, the verse is talking specifically to the person of God—to the minister, to the pastor, to the teacher—and telling him how he is to be fully equipped.

**How does that principle work itself out in the preparation of a sermon?**

Say I'm doing a series on the Epistle of Jude. It starts with that wonderful statement that we're kept by Christ, and it finishes with that wonderful doxology, "Unto him that is able to keep you from falling" (KJV). If you look at the material in the middle of the letter, the emphasis is on how we are to keep ourselves from disaster through obedience to the faith and to the standards God has laid down. There is a remarkable balance. God keeps his people; we all know that. But the letter is saying it's not enough to know God keeps you. The sign that God is keeping his people is that they're keeping themselves. That gives me a grip on the letter. It shows me what it's about, where it's going. There are some tricky and important verses in Jude I might spend a whole sermon on, but if I've got the pattern and argument of the letter, it's going to make a good deal more sense.

**When you preach on one section of a biblical book, do you still scan the entire book to bring out this melodic line?**

It's one of the most important disciplines of the preacher. It's alarming if you go to a church where a team of preachers is doing a series on Hebrews, for example, and each preacher has a different idea what the book is about. It's absolutely essential to know the way the melodic line, the argument, the theme of the book, is going.

**What are some of the secrets you've found for finding the melodic line of a book and for weaving that in and out of a sermon in a way that keeps people interested?**

That is the hard work of preparation. It is exciting to find the reason why the book was written. The difficulty is that the scholar, in writing his commentary—and of course commentaries are essential for us as part of our work—inevitably will be a detail man. He will tell you what every word means, where it comes from; he'll tell you about every dot and comma. That's fine, but I also want to know *why* it's there; and that the commentators are not usually so good at, because their scholarly skills are honed for the technical matters.

> *Finding the melodic line . . . is one of the most important disciplines of the preacher.*

If I wrote a letter to a friend saying I was catching a train and would meet him at Cambridge at three o'clock and that letter was dug up in two thousand years, the scholar would not be interested in why the letter was written. He would look at the details of the letter and write monographs on them. For example, in the letter I might have said I would call in at McDonald's on the way to Cambridge. The scholar would say, "This fellow two thousand years ago must have been a Scotsman and had Scottish friends he called in on." Then somebody else with a Ph.D. would discover McDonald's was a café. All that is interesting, but it's not what the letter was written about. The letter was written to say, "Will you meet me at three o'clock?" So the letter of 2 Peter is written to warn me that I will be carried away from my stability unless I grow in the grace and knowledge of God. That governs the whole letter. So I need to know why he wrote the letter if I'm going to look at the details.

**Do you generally find a key verse that tips you off, or is it repetition that cues you in on the key thought?**

Sometimes it is a key verse. One of the verses we used recently was Hebrews 13:8. It's what I call a kitchen calendar text: "Jesus Christ is the same yesterday and today and forever." Few people have the foggiest idea what it actually means. But it's a key to Hebrews, because it is saying that Jesus Christ, in his work as a priest and in his bringing the revelation of God, is remaining forever and ever. If the queen of England remained forever and ever, Prince Charles would never be king. So if the priest stays forever and ever, there will never be another priest. That tells me that the theme of Hebrews has to do with the finished work of Christ on the cross and that there doesn't need to be another priest, because he's the priest forever and ever. If he's a priest forever and ever, that means he's finished his redemptive and reconciling work, and there's a final message the church has been given to which nothing can be added. Hebrews begins by saying God has spoken many times in the past, but he's spoken finally by his Son.

If you put those two things together—the finished work and the final word—you have the message of Hebrews, but you're not likely to get that without going through the book and saying, what's the argument running throughout it? The writer is saying: Don't slip away from this Word. Don't add to it, because the work of Christ as a priest has been finished, and you are reconciled to God. If you're reconciled, then nobody can do anything to make you more reconciled and more acceptable.

**How do we train people to have the mental discipline to follow a line of reasoning, to get into the text and see the big picture with us?**

Most people prefer order and logic to muddle. We sometimes should say to the preacher, "Order! Order! Where are you going? What's your order?" Most people prefer the preacher to have some kind of order, so they know which direction they're meant to be going. We call that "logic on fire." That comes from Martyn Lloyd-Jones, who said the sermon should be known by its logic, but that the logic must be on fire, so it's not just cold, academic logic.

The great sermon of Paul to the Athenians is exactly that: logic on fire. It has a clear line of teaching about their ignorance and why they are ignorant and what they ought to do about it. Some people like emotional muddle, but after a while they prefer to have their mind addressed and satisfied. It's like when we were kids. We liked all the wrong food, but as we grew up, we preferred more nourishing food. As you grow up spiritually, you prefer something that nourishes your mind as well as your heart.

On Sunday I'm going to be preaching on the Ethiopian in Acts 8. When we come to a familiar story like that, we have to look at the structure the writer uses in telling the story. The writer has a hand in this and is telling the story with a point in view. Now you can use that story in a number of different ways. I read a book on personal evangelism based on the Ethiopian story, and that is legitimate. I've often kept that story up my sleeve when I've been asked at short notice to speak to businessmen, because it's a story of a businessman who met Christ. But neither of those reasons is the reason Luke tells the story. Luke tells the story because the church in Acts 8 is beginning to go out into the whole world. It's the time when the disciples are driven out of Jerusalem, first to Samaria and then to the outermost ends of the earth. So Acts 8 stands as the first chapter in that great expansion of the church out into the world. And Luke wants to tell us what is true evangelistic ministry.

Now I imagine Luke's study was pretty untidy, because he's got material coming in all the time of preaching, of campaigns, of wonderful things, of persecution, and so on. But he actually spends a whole chapter with two stories—Simon the magician, which is a false picture of ministry, and the Ethiopian and Philip, which is a true picture of ministry. So I want to know what he's got in his mind when he writes the story. He's wanting to say to me: Philip, led by the Spirit, is giving you a pattern of how to evangelize.

The first point is that the Ethiopian says to him, "How can I understand this book without a teacher?" Luke is saying the Bible is not self-explanatory, that God has appointed teachers. Then when I turn to the Pastoral Epistles, I discover only one professional qualification is needed to be a minister: he's got to be an apt teacher. So when I come back to the Ethiopian, I find it fascinating that the Holy Spirit sends Philip into the desert, into an evangelistic campaign that can't have been a very welcome invitation, where he meets one person reading a Bible he doesn't understand. The Ethiopian says to him, "Will you come up and guide me?" And the Greek word simply means "explain it; teach it to me."

So Luke is telling me that evangelism starts at understanding the Scriptures and that evangelism is not collecting scalps;

it's not getting people emotionally tied up, and it's not asking for a decision when people don't know what they're being asked to decide about. It starts with Bible teaching. It's immensely encouraging to a young minister who feels he ought to leave evangelism to the professionals when he's told, "If I teach the Bible, I'm beginning the evangelistic enterprise." That comes from looking at the structure of the story.

At Proclamation Trust we have a preaching principle called Question Time. We take that from the passage in the synoptic Gospels where Christ is under fire with questions. He often asks a question in return. In fact, occasionally he says, "I won't answer your question until you answer mine: where did John the Baptist get his authority from?" And they don't want to answer it, so he says he won't answer either. What we learn is that the preacher is not there primarily to answer the questions people have; he's primarily there to present the questions God is asking us.

When I was ministering at universities, I used to be pushed up against the wall by students, and they used to batter me with questions. God was in the dock. The impression was that if I could tell them why God had made the world in such a rotten way, they might possibly presume to believe in him. That is a completely wrong way to go about Christian apologetics. God is not in the dock. It is we who are in the dock. My job as a preacher is to bring to people's attention the great questions God asks that they would never hear otherwise.

When I was preaching to yuppies in London, many of whom in their twenties were beginning to make a great deal of money, I asked them questions like "What shall it profit a man to gain the whole world and lose his soul?" I would simply put before them a profit-and-loss account and say, "I can gain the whole world. I can take over Harrods. I can take over the Bank of England. I can become a multimillionaire and then die and lose my soul and go to hell eternally. Where is the profit in that?" They never had anybody put that question to them before. That question that God asks us in Christ's words is infinitely more important than a question they might ask me, which is largely a result of their ignorance, because they've not sat under Bible teaching.

So in Question Time we're trying to say the church ought to be on the front foot, not the back foot—not because we want to be proud or difficult, but because actually we are the people in the dock, and God is the one who is asking the questions. The preacher needs to know his responsibility.

Take Psalm 2. It begins with that magnificent question: why do the rulers and kings of the earth unite together and rage against the Lord and his anointed? That's not a question anybody ever asks. The questions we ask and that are in our daily paper are, why do the Palestinians and Jews fight against each other, and why can't we stop them? That's an important question. That's not the question the Bible is asking. The Bible is asking, why is the world fighting against God? "Well," says Mr. Jones, listening to that, "I never knew it was." We can then go on to the New Testament and show that we are all by nature not apathetic toward God but antagonistic. You and I didn't learn that until the Holy Spirit began to teach us what an enemy we've got in our own hearts toward God. But you soon learn that as a pastor or a Christian worker, because you talk to people about Christian things and find an enormous hostility whenever the thing comes close to them. Psalm 2:1 raises that great question, which people would never otherwise hear.

**Dick Lucas** served as rector of St. Helen's Church in Bishopsgate, England, for thirty-seven years.

# 4

# SPEAK TO THE ROCK

*Five signs that a sermon does not take the text seriously.*

*John Henry Beukema*

Moses was desperate. He was a preacher without a sermon, and it was Saturday night. There was no water, and the people blamed him.

Leadership for this massive group of refugees was no picnic in the best of times. In the desert with nothing to drink, it was unbearable. With Miriam recently dead, Moses faced a mutinous crowd accompanied only by Aaron. He needed a word from God—a solution.

The brothers approached Yahweh as one should—prostrate. "Moses and Aaron went from the assembly to the entrance to the Tent of Meeting and fell facedown, and the glory of the LORD appeared to them" (Num. 20:6).

Moses saw the glory. He heard the Word. He experienced the flash and the bang of the Divine. Moses came seeking an answer, and God gave one. "Take the staff, and you and your brother Aaron gather the assembly together. Speak to that rock before their eyes, and it will pour out its water. You will bring water out of the rock for the community so they and their livestock can drink" (20:8).

Moses chose not to preach that Word. Yes, he preached a word, but it was not the one given for the occasion. "So Moses took the staff from the LORD's presence, just as he commanded him. He and Aaron gathered the assembly together in front of the rock and Moses said to them, 'Listen, you rebels, must we bring you water out of this rock?' Then Moses raised his arm and struck the rock twice with his staff. Water gushed out, and the community and their livestock drank" (20:9–11).

Moses struck the rock when he was only to speak to it. He struck the rock because it had worked so well last time (Exod. 17:1–7). He struck the rock because the rebels incited him to action. He struck the rock because the community needed water. He struck the rock, and it worked. So what was wrong with the word Moses preached? It was more than the little detail of methodology. The great prophet did not take the text seriously. He followed a previous command. To strike the rock was to obey God—the first time. But this time he reacted, instead of listening to and communicating the truth.

Moses filled an obvious and urgent need but missed the objective. The main purpose was to honor Yahweh as holy. The point was to hear, obey, and communicate the divine Word as he received it. In that, Moses failed, and it cost him.

That should fill us with holy fear. We who claim to speak for God, we who announce good news, must take note. Yahweh's primary concern is not results but obedience. Yahweh cares more about being quoted properly and having his Word applied correctly than about immediate effectiveness.

The staff was Moses' to use. That was the stick of authority. God told him to take it with him to the waiting assembly (20:8).

He was to bring the staff into the pulpit. Moses obeyed in that (20:9). But it went from symbol to club. It changed from a divine instrument to a human weapon. Life-giving water resulted, but violence was done to the rock—and to the Word.

It is a simple thing to preach a sermon that is inspiring but not inspired; effective but not authentic. As we stand to speak for God, how certain we must be that we deliver the Word.

Here are five signs that a sermon does not take the text seriously.

## We give the butter to the baby

I watched as the young mother left her husband in charge of their baby and went to the restaurant restroom. "Now, don't let her get anything from the table," she said in parting.

With mom out of the room, the baby spied the nicely wrapped pats of butter and started reaching. Dad refused, and baby started to scream. A few ear-piercing seconds later, Dad handed over the butter. What wasn't eaten was squished between fingers and smeared on her hair, but things were quieter—at least until mom returned.

That is what Moses did. The people organized a resistance effort. Gathering in opposition, they *quarreled* with the leadership. This word is used in Exodus 21:18 to describe a fight that leads to a disabling injury. The crowd confronted and complained, and Moses was motivated to mollify. Their noisy demands created an urgency overriding the Word to be preached. Moses and Aaron listened to the clamor of the people over the voice of Yahweh. God's commentary on their actions was that "when the community rebelled . . . both of you disobeyed my command to honor me as holy before their eyes" (Num. 27:14).

Ben Patterson lists one of the temptations of a preacher as trying "to turn stones into bread, to give people what they want instead of what they need." The willingness to sacrifice accurate interpretation for numerical effectiveness, truth for trends, has dire consequences. When things get noisy, we must make certain we are not placating but proclaiming. The sermon aimed at quelling the rebellion may not take seriously the real Word.

## We MacGyver a sermon

The Learning Channel is home to a show called *Junkyard Wars*. Teams compete against each other in building a functional submarine or cannon or motorboat or whatever. They do it from parts they cannibalize from a junkyard. Ingeniously teams may take the engine from a lawnmower and make an airplane.

It takes skill to use something in a way it was not intended. But it is not something to admire when it comes to preaching. It may be entertaining, even awe inspiring, but it endangers truth. Moses took a truth from one place and forced it into another. A tragic difference. God defined the misapplication as disobedience. In both Exodus 17 and Numbers 20, water was needed, and a rock was involved, but the purposes were slightly different. Exodus 17 answered the question, "Is the LORD among us or not?" (v. 7). In Numbers 20 the issue is trusting Yahweh enough to honor him as holy in the sight of the Israelites (v. 12).

Textual misapplication is a danger in all preaching, but most especially when the preaching is topical. We can use words from Scripture but violate their meaning in context.

Don Sunukjian states that topical preaching can be truly biblical if the preacher doesn't make "a passage speak about a subject other than the one intended by the biblical writer." The only way to guard against that is to do the hard work necessary to know the context of all texts used. Otherwise you may manipulate the text to fit your purpose.

Topical sermons may not be bad sermons, nor unbiblical, but many are MacGyvered together to accomplish what the preacher saw as true.

## We show ears but no elephant

In critiquing one sermon, author Kent Edwards wrote, "The sermon *is* biblical in that it is true to Scripture in general. But it is not biblical in that it does not express the original scriptural author's (Paul's) main idea." This is where sermons easily go wrong. They make a point, or several, and what is said is true. But the sermon is not authentic and authoritative if that is not the point of the text. Fragments of a text can be put forward, without generating a biblical sermon, if those fragments are not true to the context. There is an ear here, or a tail there, but the elephant never makes it into the picture.

The big idea must flow demonstrably from the sermon text. Unless the authority of any point, or sermon theme, comes from the text given in support, the authority comes only from the preacher. If the word preached does not truly arise from that text, it is not the Word. The average congregant might never know the difference, but the preacher must.

In Numbers 20 Moses subtly presents himself as the authority in front of the people. He rebukes them as rebels, and says, "Must we bring you water out of this rock?" (v. 10). This word for "bring" or "fetch" is causative. Moses says, "Do we have to deliver again?" "Shall we bring another rabbit out of the hat for you?"

In his four-hundred-year-old classic book on preaching, William Perkins writes, "Interpretation is the opening up of the words and statements of Scripture in order to bring out its single, full and natural sense." An ear will not do. Our sermons carry a weightier authority when they show the whole elephant.

## We carve away everything that is not a duck

I tried carving as a hobby—for a while. I found it increasingly difficult to carve because of the bandages. My tools were sharp and my skills dull, resulting in a plethora of incidental incisions. I looked at one log and envisioned a goose masterpiece. I created the pattern, affixed it to the block and began to chisel. I began removing everything that didn't fit the pattern. Trapped inside was a goose longing for freedom. Then I lopped off too much. A whole goose was no longer possible. Now I saw a duck. He's still in there somewhere.

There are certain approaches to Scripture reading that make me smile and cringe simultaneously. For example, "Our text this morning is from Psalm 68:1–5; 19–20; 28; 32–35." What is missing are most of the hard words. "Surely God will crush the heads of his enemies." "Plunge your feet in the blood of your foes, while the tongues of your dogs have their share." There are many pleasant words in that chapter, but they are mingled with brutal ones.

To extract the perceived nuggets from the "slag," leaves you with a different word. We cannot go to a text and strip away everything that does not fit what we want to say or feel good saying. If we present a text with no seeds, with all warts air-brushed out, sanitized for a modern congregation, then we have not taken the text seriously.

A sermon that takes a text seriously at least acknowledges elements in the text that do not fit the theme of the sermon. It accounts for, and/or deals with, all the verses in the sermon text. If we approach the text with that intent, with that openness, it will say things that we never see otherwise. Those things become uniquely powerful.

A sermon takes the text seriously when it does not come to the text with a duck pattern in hand. It is too easy for us to whittle away whatever does not fit our preconception and our nagging need. When that happens, we make the word instead of allowing the Word to make us.

## We pay too little attention to the one behind the curtain

Scripture is God's revelation of himself, his gospel, and his will for our lives. In preaching we pull aside the curtain to show more of him through his Word. Sermons that are all about us and little about God do not take the text seriously.

At the least, be very suspicious if week after week the big idea of your sermons don't have God in them. The preacher's task is to ask, what does this text say to us about God? And how does this text impact the lives of my people? Sometimes those two questions are not only related, they are also the same thing. But we must address them both. Moses did not. In this sermon, he failed on the God thing.

Most preachers do a good job of self-mutilation after giving a sermon. Most feel the sharp sting of people's criticism from time to time. Yet how bad would it be to have God attack your sermon? Yahweh said, "You blew it, Moses." That must have produced the worst ever Monday-morning-after.

The failure was for the worst of all reasons. We get balled up over a poor illustration, a misspoken word, or an uninspired delivery. Moses received the most horrific of homiletic censures: "You did not trust in me enough to honor me as holy in the sight of the Israelites" (20:12). All other failings pale in comparison. What else matters? How many times have I done the same? The sermon was effective; stuff happened; the delivery was passionate and powerful; but it wasn't the Word. God must show himself holy through the preaching. We must take the text seriously for that to happen.

Taking the Bible seriously requires that we trust God. Trust that the truth will be revealed through hard work and obedience. Trust that our courage to speak it will bring the results he desires. Trust that the Word will be relevant to the hearer, even more than the word we could construct ourselves. As Haddon Robinson says, "Something can always happen when a preacher takes God's Word seriously."

*Taking the Bible seriously requires that we trust God.*

**John Henry Beukema** is pastor of King Street Church in Chambersburg, Pennsylvania, and author of *Stories from God's Heart* (Moody). He served as associate editor of PreachingToday.com.

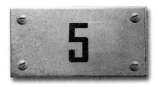

# 5

# PREACHING PARABLES

*Do you have the literary skills to interpret this unique genre?*

*Craig Blomberg*

*Interpreting the parables of Jesus is one of the ultimate tests of any preacher. In this interview we draw on the expertise of scholar Craig Blomberg, author of* Preaching the Parables.

**What are your favorite parables and why?**

Simply because certain parables, like the Prodigal Son and the Good Samaritan, are used so often, I have come to appreciate some of the lesser-cited passages. Because of my heart for good stewardship, I appreciate texts like the Rich Man and Lazarus and, in Luke 16, the Unjust Steward. That particular parable for many people seems to be the most puzzling of all.

**One major question about interpreting and preaching parables is whether the parables of Jesus are meant to give us one message or many. What do you believe about that issue?**

There have been wild pendulum swings throughout the history of the church in interpreting the parables, and, as with many controversies, the truth often falls somewhere in between. In my studies I have tried to go back before the era of all of the Greek and Roman allegorizing of parables and other biblical narratives to the way parables of the Jewish rabbis were taken. Some of them might have been Jesus' contemporaries. Typically there were two or three or maybe four, but seldom more, key characters or details that clearly did have symbolic significance. Seldom were narrative stories of considerable detail narrowed down to just one main point; on the other hand, it was seldom if ever the case that more than just a handful of key details had symbolism to them. The approach I have developed argues that while one may seek a big idea or a unifying proposition for a sermon, when one unpacks that in terms of the parables, one should understand how many main characters there are and what their relationship is. Usually one is able to find a key lesson or subpoint based on each of those characters.

**How do you carry that off effectively in a sermon? Do you tell the story three different ways, one for each character?**

That's one option. A study on the Prodigal Son, tucked away in an esoteric scholarly journal, did precisely that—three consecutive readings of the Prodigal, from the eyes of the wayward son and then the older brother and finally the waiting father. The conclusion was that the one main point of the story was that repentance is always possible no matter how far you have fallen, and one should not begrudge God's generosity to the wayward, but recognize that God is loving, wishing

> *There have been wild pendulum swings throughout the history of the church in interpreting the parables.*

that lost sons near and far should return. When I read the end of the article, I said, "That's exactly what the parable means, but this guy can't count. That's not one point; that's three. One point for each of the main characters."

But one doesn't have to structure the sermon that way. If people are used to a more typical three-point or three-subpoint message, oftentimes successive episodes of the passage will focus on a different character in turn, and so you can combine traditional exposition moving sequentially through the passage with a focus on the different characters.

There may be other times where you want to do more classic, big-idea preaching and try to take those three prongs and combine them together. Take the parable of the two sons in Matthew 21, which seems to many people like the same structured story as the Prodigal minus most of the detail. A vineyard owner tells his two sons to go to work, and one day the one says he will but he doesn't, and the other says he won't but he does. I had a colleague who suggested a big idea for that passage as "performance takes priority over promise." In the three *P* words, you have the three prongs of the passage summarized succinctly. I've never been able to come up with something like that for a text as rich in detail as the Prodigal Son.

**How many parables have a multiplicity of characters contributing to the main points of the story?**

There's no agreement on exactly how many parables of Jesus there are, but most estimates put the figure somewhere around forty. Roughly two-thirds of those can be classified as triangular in structure, where there is a master figure—a God, a father, a shepherd, a slave owner—and then contrasting subordinates or sometimes groups of subordinates such as sons or servants or slaves or sheep or seeds. There is usually a striking contrast between those subordinates: a good example, bad example. Often, though not always, there is a radical surprise as to who turns out to be the good example versus who turns out to be the bad example. About two-thirds of all of Jesus' parables are structured that way.

Another one-sixth have a master figure and a solitary subordinate, or simply two contrasting figures without a master, and they seem to me to fall nicely into two-point structures. The final six tend to be the shortest of the parables, in which the conventional wisdom of one main point seems to work well.

**So the number of primary characters should help determine the structure of the sermon.**

That is my contention.

**What about those parables with parallels in more than one gospel where we have somewhat differing details? How do we handle those differences?**

First determine if what at first glance appear to be parallels are in fact genuine parallels. There are at least three pairs of particularly well known parables—the so-called Great Banquet in Luke 14 and the Wedding Feast in Matthew 22, the two versions of the Lost Sheep in Matthew 18 and Luke 15, and the Talents in Matthew 25 and Pounds in Luke 19—where, if we believe the text is inspired and accurate and we pay close attention to the context of those passages, we have to come to the conclusion that Jesus is telling a similar story to what he has told on a separate occasion in a different place at a different stage in his ministry. While it is interesting to compare the similarities between the two, I don't believe we can use the one in interpreting the other.

In the remaining instances, it does seem we have genuine parallels. If one is preaching sequentially through a particular gospel, it is important—whether we're talking about parables or any other portion—to do as little comparative work in the other Gospels as we can get by with. There may be something that's necessary to fill out the historical setting or background, but our goal as interpreters preaching a series through Luke—when we get to Luke 20, for example, and the Parable of the Wicked Tenants, which does appear in Matthew and Mark as well—is to look for what Luke saw as the key things he wanted to emphasize in light of the rest of his gospel. The danger for preachers is that we don't preach the Bible, what God inspired; we preach an artificial harmony binding texts together. On the other hand, if somebody is preaching a series on parables, or maybe a series on texts on stewardship and along the way you throw in a couple of parables, then it's more legitimate to draw in some of the parallel accounts to see what light they shed on the text at hand.

**As with any Scripture, we can read into a text all kinds of later New Testament theology that the original hearers didn't have, misinterpret it, or not give the text at hand the weight it needs to have. Preachers must guard against putting together two parables that really aren't the same. We don't want to create a harmony of the parables.**

Yes. You combine together two concerns there, and I would agree with both of them. The first concern is the one we talked about a minute ago, but then you also alluded to an equally important concern, and that is not to go beyond Jesus into historically later developments in the New Testament and interpret Jesus, say, in light of Paul. It's at times legitimate to do the reverse, particularly if we have reason to believe Paul is alluding to a teaching of Jesus. But it obviously would not be legitimate historically to try to make sense of what Jesus could have expected an audience in Galilee in the first third of the first century to have understood from his words by appealing to something written twenty years later to Corinth.

**As we interpret and preach the parables, what are some of the other do's and don'ts of dealing with allegory or symbolic stories?**

Scholarly consensus, particularly in the first half of the twentieth century, swung the pendulum too far away from the rampant allegorization of so much of church history. That's understandable because trends that take issues to extreme are often met by overreactions in the opposite direction. Nevertheless I would much rather have a preacher err on the side of caution, preaching one central point without much or any allegory, than to revert back to the opposite extreme that still dominates preaching throughout the world. In my experience and travels, that is particularly true in the second and third worlds where many pastors have had no formal education. Better to preach just one point even if you miss a couple than to come up with elaborate hidden significance from every last detail.

**Any interesting examples?**

In the parables of either the talents or pounds, you have the faithful servants followed by a faithless servant who has done nothing with his master's money and is consigned to outer darkness, where there will be weeping and gnashing of teeth. In the historical context, Jesus is speaking to Jewish followers of his who are part of God's chosen people, who are part of the entire community of Israel, all of whom believe that they are within the covenant. His point is to challenge them by saying:

Not all of you who think you are in are truly in. In fact, a time is quickly coming when you won't be in at all unless you are my followers.

Because people miss that, they jump immediately to the allegorical equation that every time you see a servant in a parable it must stand for a Christian. Now, you have a faithless servant who is thrown into a place of darkness and weeping and gnashing of teeth. If you're an Arminian, that's not a problem, because you just lost your salvation. But if you're a Calvinist, this creates greater problems. To explain it, some preachers say there must be some compartment in heaven for people who just barely get in by the skin of their teeth. It's not the most pleasant part of heaven, because there is outer darkness and weeping and gnashing of teeth. My reaction is, "Wait a minute. Do you really believe this? Folks, that's hell. Now, let's figure out what you did wrong in interpreting the parable."

**When you preached the Parable of the Pharisee and the Tax Collector from Luke 18, you titled it "The Parable of the Recovering Homosexual." What were you hoping to accomplish with that title?**

Some shock. Some interest. Some curiosity. That tends to be one of the better-known shorter parables of Jesus. Pharisees are supposedly understood by just about anyone in our culture today. You don't have to be a churchgoer to have in your vocabulary *pharisaic* as an adjective that means legalistic, hypercritical, hypocritical—but that's exactly not what the average Jew in the first century would ever have thought of when they heard of Pharisees. These were by far the most beloved of the various Jewish leadership sects in Jesus' day. Jesus shocked his audiences when he pointed out the hypocrisy of particular groups of

Pharisaic leaders. I needed to come up with a different counterpart to Pharisees.

And I needed to do the same for tax collectors, because today a tax collector is an impersonal computerized form. It doesn't create the dynamic of someone who is working for the hated, occupying, military imperial forces of Rome. It doesn't create the dynamic of someone whose reputation was that he made his living by charging vastly higher sums of money than he turned over to his superiors. I looked for a contemporary equivalent to someone who is very hated and despised, even by well-respected, contemporary religious, conservative insiders. I don't know of any better example than the ongoing tension in the evangelical community between most practicing homosexuals and a huge percentage of conservative Christians and leaders, at least if we are to judge by the rhetoric.

What one is attempting to do in contemporizing a parable is to re-create in the culture of one's audience the identical impact that Jesus' original story would have had, by examining each detail and asking if it carries the same impact. Look for a contemporary setting where a cluster of details could, as closely as possible, approximate that same impact.

**Have you seen this contemporizing done in ways that are not legitimate?**

The biggest danger is that one doesn't do one's historical homework carefully enough. As with all narrative preaching on any biblical genre, more time is usually required. The benefits are usually enormous, and it is rare that a well-crafted narrative sermon does not meet with incredible response and appreciation by those who are open to its message. The danger is that one will come up with modern equivalents that really aren't true equivalents at all.

An example that comes to mind deals with the preaching in the marketplaces that occurs in the book of Acts so consistently. People don't understand that news was disseminated by a daily courier coming to the town square. Even in the smallest village in the ancient Roman Empire, a courier gave the news at least once a day. This was the place where people went to buy their foodstuffs for the day in a world without refrigeration. It was also a place where, unlike our supermarkets, people expected to go and meet their friends and socialize.

If we go to shopping malls today and do outdoor evangelism, more often than not we will not be reproducing the dynamic or the intentions of the biblical world, even though we think we are literally following their example. The closer parallels today would be writing letters to the editor of the newspaper, speaking on college campuses—which are key places of social and political preparation for actions groups of various kinds—and creating inroads into secular radio and television talk shows. We need to be more creative and at the same time more historical as we draw these correspondences from the ancient world to today.

### How do you interpret and preach the Parable of the Unjust Steward, or Shrewd Manager, from Luke 16?

In Luke 16:1–9 there are three statements—two in verse 8 and one in verse 9—that seem to align exactly with the three prongs of that particular parable. That is not a triangular structure but simply a straight top-down model. If you were to think of it in terms of modern company flowcharts, it has a master, a servant underneath that master, and then that steward who is manager of his master's estate has various debtors underneath his authority. The master praised the unjust steward for his shrewdness. Then you have the somewhat ironic but often true aside that the children of light often are not as shrewd in their dealings as the children of this world are in theirs.

Finally you have the command, in cryptic fashion, to make friends by means of the tainted material possessions of this world, so that when this life and all of its possessions fail, those people to whom you ministered or who have become believers and have preceded you to glory will welcome you into the eternal habitation. So you have the master's praise, the responsibility for shrewd discipleship on the part of those who are true servants, and then the welcome of the debtors. However one chooses to structure the sermon, your three points are sitting right there in the text to be unpacked.

### How about the Parable of the Workers in the Vineyard from Matthew 20?

That reverts back to a more triangular structure. It's a bit more complex. At first glance it seems you just have groups of workers hired at different hours of the day, but the only ones Jesus focuses on are the first hired and the last hired. So there is a master figure, the vineyard owner, and the first hired and the last hired. The dynamic is the seemingly unfair, equal treatment of all.

In verses 13–16 the master replies to the complaining servants, "Friend, I am not being unfair to you. Didn't you agree to work for a denarius? Take your pay and go. I want to give the one man was hired last the same as I gave you. Don't I have the right to do what I want with my own money? Or are you envious because I am generous?" Then Jesus concludes, "The last will be first, and the first will be last." That comment has often puzzled people, because it sounds like Jesus is treating everyone equally, so how can we then say there is a reversal? But I would argue that if they are all treated equally, he is simply saying that all positions are potentially interchangeable. The points of the parable involve the fact that God is never unjust. He is never less than fair. We probably don't want to demand God to be fair with us, because then we're basically asking him to send us to hell. His grace is entirely undeserved.

The second part of the passage stresses that God in Christ is exceedingly generous. He hasn't been less than fair with anyone in the story. All got at least what they were promised. He is simply being much more than fair with those who were hired last. With the little epigram in verse 16, there is stress on the ultimate fundamental equality of all of God's people in eternity in the fullness of the kingdom of God.

**What parables, in your estimation, are most frequently misinterpreted and why?**

I suspect throughout church history that the Good Samaritan may well have gotten more misguided press than any other. In the attempt to limit it to one point, and given our lack of creativity in thinking of contemporary equivalents, the message often becomes "we ought to stop and help the stranded motorist more often than we do."

There are all kinds of problems with that. One is simply the question of the modern equivalent. Most stranded motorists are not dying on the side of the road, as the man in the parable was. Another problem is that if there are three prongs to the parable, then imitating the love of the Samaritan is only one-third of what the passage is teaching. The point that Christian audiences probably need more is the lesson of the priest and the Levite. Oftentimes those who are consumed by religious duty either think their position excuses them from being loving in situations of spontaneous need or are simply blind to those situations altogether.

But even then I don't think an expositor has gotten to the heart of Jesus' message, which is the shock value of a wounded man being rescued by the hated enemy, the Samaritan. Unless one of my points is something like "even my enemy is my neighbor," I'm convinced we have missed the heart and genius and most central part of that passage. To contemporize the story we need to think along the lines of Americans in 2004 imagining a GI wounded in the Iraqi desert who is rescued and nursed back to health by a member of the Al Qaeda terrorist organization. If we don't get some folks upset with us, we have not re-created the dynamic of Jesus' original parable.

**How many of Jesus' parables would you say were to evoke that kind of response?**

Of those twenty-five or so passages that have three points or a pair of contrasting subordinates, at least two-thirds of the time there is a shocking reversal of who is the hero and who is the goat.

**You've intrigued me with the idea that certain parables are often misinterpreted and therefore mispreached. Do you think of another parable that, because of our cultural distance, we miss the point, we miss the surprise, and we mispreach?**

The next one that comes to mind is the Rich Man and Lazarus, because so many conservative Christians are consumed with interest in eschatology. Precisely because there is so little in the Scriptures that directly impinges on that topic, people turn to this parable even though they agree it should not be allegorized.

Even though there are other details that they would never want to teach doctrinally, such as people in heaven who will want to go to hell. Nevertheless, because it looks like a text that could refer to some kind of agony that unbelievers experience after death and before the general resurrection, that passage gets used to support that.

Just about any major recent commentary on either Luke or the parables will point out that Jesus undoubtedly was aware of a number of Jewish parallels to that story. What was different about his account has to do with the way the story ends, where there is no travel from one part of the afterlife to another. People's fates are irrevocably sealed, and even if someone were raised from the dead, it wouldn't make a bit of difference, because the rich man was a Jew who knew the Torah; he knew his responsibilities; he had paid no attention to God during his life anyway.

To say we can come up with doctrinal teaching about the nature of the afterlife from this parable violates principles that most of these same expositors would follow everywhere else.

**Craig Blomberg** is professor of New Testament at Denver Seminary in Denver, Colorado, and author of *Preaching the Parables* (Baker Academic).

# 6

# SOUL SERMONS FROM PSALMS

*How a sermon from Psalms can touch the heart like the psalm itself.*

*Kenneth W. Smith*

The Psalms possess tremendous power to impact us. They reach past the surface concerns and emotional defenses of our daily lives and open our hearts toward God. Depending upon which psalm is in view, a given psalm may comfort our hearts, lift our feelings toward God, convict our consciences of sin, or arouse us out of our complacency.

This phenomenon is no accident. From beginning to end—from the process of composition to the time of our reading and reflection upon a psalm—God's Spirit takes an active role in the process. Each psalm is carefully shaped by both its divine and human authors to address us in specific ways. Allender and Longman write: "No section of the Bible teaches us the language of the soul better than the Psalms, which reflect the movement of the human heart in rich, evocative, and startling language. In a voice that disrupts, invites, and reveals, the psalmist draws us to the voice of God."[1]

God's Spirit prepared the biblical authors to write, and he prepares our hearts and minds to read and understand. We cannot uncover the mysteries of the Spirit's inner workings as God reveals himself to contemporary believers when they read or listen to a particular psalm. Much of what goes on when a person *receives* a message from God's Word lies beyond human understanding. However, we may be able to look behind the veil to discern some of the Spirit's work on the other end of God's self-revealing work. It is possible to analyze the Psalms themselves to discern the particular means by which God has acted to *transmit* his Word to readers and listeners. Yet, Tremper Longman cautions, "The trick is to learn how to read poetry in a way that respects its original, heart-targeted intention without doing so much analysis that we suck the life out of it."[2]

With Longman's concern duly noted, our aim as preachers should still be to uncover the methods by which the psalmists employed tools from a carefully prepared poetic genre in order to shape and transmit God's word. A carefully executed poetic and rhetorical analysis is important with a psalm intended for use as a preaching text. Just as each psalm is designed in specific ways to maximize its impact on readers and listeners, our sermons can be similarly crafted.

It is true that we must approach sermon design with great care lest we succumb to the temptation to manipulate our listeners' emotions. Our primary goal is not to produce an emotional response in our hearers. Rather, we should aim to communicate and apply God's Word accurately and effectively to listeners' lives.

However, an attempt to reproduce some of a psalm's built-in rhetorical effects does not undermine the text's accuracy. To the contrary, we need to ask ourselves why so many sermons empty the preaching text of its own innate poetic and rhetorical character. If a psalm from which we intend to preach has within it the power to comfort or convict, challenge, provoke, reassure, or to bow or lift a listener's heart and mind in praise toward an awesome God, shouldn't a sermon on that same psalm produce a similar effect?

Different types of literature call for different homiletical approaches. Rather than use a one-size-fits-all sermon form to preach from the Psalms, why not seek to work in concert with the psalmists themselves? We would do well to mimic some of the effects of a psalm in our sermon by use of rhetorical devices and strategies that are inherent in the genre of Hebrew poetry.

Thomas Long makes the case for carefully examining the rhetorical dynamics of a biblical text. He maintains that it is possible to design our sermons to "say and do what the text says and does in its setting."[3]

Obviously, we will not be able to carry over 100 percent of a psalm's poetic power into our sermons. If that were our goal, we would only have to read the psalm to our congregation and sit down. Sermons have become a form unto themselves, with their own purposes and rhetorical strategies. Lives have been touched by sermons in which little attention has been paid to the use of poetic rhetorical devices. However, new developments in the area of rhetorical criticism have supplied us with a new appreciation and awareness of the inspiration and ingenuity with which the biblical psalmists conducted their craft. If we continue to stuff the Psalms into traditional didactic sermon forms, we will be much like the proverbial father assembling his child's bicycle on Christmas Eve without following the directions. Our sermons will have many leftover parts for which we can find no use.

And—although our sermon will be functional—it will probably never move with the power and grace that it might have had.

Rhetorical analysis should not replace exegesis. Rather, it should supplement our exegetical study of a psalm and build upon it. Exegesis answers the question, what is the psalmist saying? Rhetorical analysis answers the questions, how did the psalmist say it, and what specifically causes this psalm to affect me the way it does? Exegesis reads what a given line says. Rhetorical criticism seeks to uncover from the same line(s) how the text may be affecting readers or listeners while they are receiving the contents of the message.[4]

When performing a rhetorical analysis on the Psalms, it would be wonderful if we could find a single key that would unlock the secret behind the beauty and power of poetry in general and the Psalter in particular. Poetic discourse often soars far above plain discourse in terms of the relative effects produced within listeners. Why does "Four score and seven years ago our forefathers brought forth . . ." touch us in a way that "Eighty-seven years ago our ancestors instituted . . ." does not? If we could grasp the reason why the former soars while the latter merely plods along in the same general direction, then we could develop a simple formula that would vitalize our preaching on any given psalm.

I haven't found a master key. What I've found instead is an entire key ring with different-shaped keys that unlock different types of locks. There are different types of psalms just as there are different types of locks. What makes one psalm affect us deeply often differs from what makes another psalm affect us. Preachers who wish to unlock the rhetorical power of a psalm and carry some of that power over into their sermons will need to carry a full key chain. Sometimes we will have to try several keys in a lock before we find just the right one.

This is because the Psalter employs a multitude of rhetorical strategies. Which strategy is used and to what degree in a given psalm makes a great difference in the impact the psalm may have upon readers and listeners. Therefore, as we apply the following questions to a given psalm, note that one question may be more useful than another in the rhetorical analysis.

## Fourteen questions to ask about a psalm

Below are fourteen questions to ask of any psalm, which I will use to analyze Psalm 8. This psalm is a hymn celebrating the greatness of God as Creator of all things. It is quoted by the author of Hebrews, who identifies "the son of man" in verse 4 of the psalm as Jesus. It would probably be better to preach two sermons, one on Psalm 8 and the other on Hebrews 2, rather than to preach one complex and lengthy sermon on the two texts paired together. The rhetorical analysis that follows deals primarily with Psalm 8 as it functioned in its original literary context.

> *Preachers who wish to unlock the rhetorical power of a psalm and carry some of that power over into their sermons will need to carry a full key chain.*

1. **To what genre does this psalm belong?[5] How is it similar to other psalms of the same genre? How, if at all, does it differ?**

Psalm 8 is a hymn. The purpose of a hymn is to give praise to God for something. In this case God is to be praised for his work as Creator and for his ongoing care of his creatures, especially human beings. The psalmist opens the song with words of praise uttered directly to God. This psalm differs from many other hymns in that the psalmist's opening words are addressed to God directly rather than to other worshipers, as is the case with hymns such as Psalms 95, 96, and 100.

2. **What mood(s), subject matter, and intended effects are usually characteristic of a psalm of this type? Does this psalm remain true to type?**

Hymns typically convey a joyous mood. This psalm celebrates God's work as Creator of the world. By casting his eye toward the heavens, the psalmist paints a picture of the grandeur and vastness of God and his handiwork. Then, in the middle of the psalm, he shifts the focus down to how small and insignificant we are by comparison. He does this with a question: "What is man that you are mindful of him, the son of man that you care for him?" Humanity is elevated to a place of prominence in the next verse in language that calls to mind the theology of creation in Genesis 1.

3. **How well does this psalm follow the usual structural patterns of psalms of this type? Does the author introduce any innovations that alter the psalm's rhetorical impact?**

Hymns typically open and close with words of praise. The body of the hymn offers reasons for praise. Psalm 8 contains both of these features. The opening and closing verses operate as a type of refrain. The strategic placement of a question in the middle of the psalm deepens the sense of wonder and awe at the glory of God's power and the intimacy of his concern for us.

4. **Are the psalm's contents arranged inductively or deductively? What evidence points in this direction?**

The psalm has a deductive feeling, because the psalmist opens the hymn with words of praise. He presents the desired response from listeners at the outset and supports the call for worship with reasons to do so. This contrasts with psalms such as Psalm 130, which has an inductive feeling because it opens with the words, "Out of the depths I cry to you."

5. **What is the rhetorical effect of this psalm? What feelings does it produce in me as a reader? How does the psalmist achieve these effects?**

The psalm makes me feel small by comparison to the grandeur of the night sky. I have a similar feeling when I stand looking at the ocean and think about the vastness and power it contains. The psalmist achieves the effect by sharply shifting the focus from the heavens to human beings.

6. **What is the psalm's emotional topography? Where are the highs, lows, and level places emotionally? What is the psalmist saying when the psalm hits these different levels of emotion?**

The psalm opens in a major key, shifts momentarily to a minor key via the question posed in verse 4, and shifts back to a major key with the answer to his question in verse 5.

7. **What is the psalmist's point of view in time or space? How does the psalmist's point of view contribute to the psalm's message and effect? Is there a spatial or temporal movement within this psalm? If so, what effect does this produce?**[6]

It's as if the psalmist is standing outside on a starlit night, gazing upward to the heavens and musing about the greatness of the One who is above the heavens. At some point during his meditation, it is possible, although not certain, that he hears a baby cry (something calls to his mind the image of a very young child). His focus shifts from the grandeur of the heavens downward to the smallness and seeming insignificance of the human race. Yet the psalmist is aware of humanity's elevated position by God's design. He says humanity is "lower than the heavenly beings, yet crowned with glory and honor . . . ruler over the works of [God's] hands." At this point, the psalmist appears to have a panoramic view of the creatures that inhabit the land, sea, and sky.

**8. What is the psalm's narrative plot, if any?[7]**

Narrative plot appears to contribute less to the rhetorical effect of this psalm than to many other psalms. What plot there is has to do mostly with creation.

**9. What key images are in the psalm? What makes them key? How does the psalmist develop the images? What effect do they produce?**

Suckling infants, enemies and avengers, God placing the sun, moon, and stars in the heavens, human beings, heavenly beings, flocks, herds, birds, and fish are all present in this brief hymn. The purpose behind the inclusion of suckling infants, enemies, and avengers seems somewhat unclear. Their mention does seem to add a note of sublimity. The juxtaposition of humanity against the vastness of the rest of creation inspires a sense of awe and quiet reflection.

**10. How, if at all, does the psalmist build tension into the psalm? How does he relieve it?**

The only significant tension comes in the middle of the psalm, with the psalmist's age-old question about the significance of humanity in the larger scheme of things. He relieves the tension immediately in the next verse by answering his own question.

**11. What kind of language does the psalmist use? Is it concrete or abstract? What effect does it have?**

The psalmist uses language and develops themes that call to mind the opening chapters of Genesis. The psalmist uses concrete and specific words rather than abstract ones.

**12. What poetic devices does the psalmist employ? These may include such things as imagery, metaphors, similes, personification, hyperbole, apostrophe, shifting or unusual tenses, the presence or absence of refrains, and the like. What effect do these produce?[8]**

The psalmist does not employ many of the poetic devices found commonly throughout the Psalter. For instance, he does not use metaphors, similes, or hyperbole. He does use refrains, but only at the beginning and end of the psalm. These are praises given in the form of direct address to God. He also uses highly visual and concrete imagery and jumps freely from one image to another.

**13. What are some of the intensifying features, if any, within this psalm?**

In a couple of places, the psalmist begins with a general term and then amplifies the term by mentioning a few specific terms that fit under it. The word *heavens* is amplified by "work of your fingers," "moon," and "stars." "Everything under his feet" is amplified by "flocks and herds," "birds of the air," and "fish of the sea."

**14. What is the psalmist attempting to do in or through this psalm? What does he want the reader to think, feel, believe, or do as a result of reading this psalm?[9]**

The psalmist wants worshipers to praise God for the glory of his handiwork. He also wants worshipers to come away from singing the psalm with a combination of humility and feelings of exultation at our unique standing in this vast universe.

## Ways to preach from Psalm 8

As we move to shaping a sermon based on Psalm 8, we are interested especially in how it functions rhetorically. What effect does the psalm produce on the listener, and how does the psalmist achieve that effect? How may we carry over some of this rhetorical impact to a contemporary audience? What moves will we make? What kinds of illustrations would be compatible with the biblical text?

Psalm 8 is one of a small group of psalms devoted to the topic of creation. One striking thing about this psalm is the sharp rhetorical turn the psalmist makes in the middle of the psalm. He begins in verses 1 and 3 by using broad brushstrokes to paint a verbal picture of God's creation of the universe. He depicts God's glory by the vastness of the heavens in which he has placed the moon and stars. In verse 4 the psalmist makes a sudden rhetorical turn. Without warning he shifts to a question: "What is man that you are mindful of him, the son of man that you care for him?" The sharp juxtaposition of this question with the glory of God displayed in the heavens is the key to understanding and preaching the entire psalm.

We could begin the sermon by heightening the hearer's sense of the grandeur of the creation. In a personal approach, we could describe an experience of the feeling that the psalmist captures in the opening verses: "When I was a child, I once tried to count the stars. . . ." Another approach might be to expand upon the psalmist's observations with an illustration from science: "If only the psalmist had had a telescope to survey the night sky. . . ." We could then describe facts about the size of the universe, the number of galaxies and stars, and the like. Our goal is to intensify the feeling of awe at the majesty of the creation. The more this feeling of awe comes across in the sermon, the more effective will be the transition into the next major move.

In a transition to the next move, we could pose the psalmist's question: "Is it any wonder that David asked, 'What is man that you are mindful of him, the son of man that you care for him?' How small and seemingly insignificant we feel when we compare ourselves with the heavens!" At this point, our feeling of insignificance could be heightened with a quotation from an author such as Carl Sagan: "As long as there have been humans we have searched for our place in the cosmos. Where are we? Who are we? We find that we live on an insignificant planet of a humdrum star lost in a galaxy tucked away in some forgotten corner of a universe in which there are far more galaxies than people."[10]

The effect of the illustration could be further heightened by repeating the adjectives and nouns from the quotation: *insignificant planet . . . humdrum star . . . forgotten corner of the universe.* Are we really "insignificant" and "forgotten"? We could offer an illustration on feelings of insignificance using salient quotations, studies that have been done concerning people's sense of insignificance, or a story from everyday life.

To stay with the emotional and thematic contours of the psalm, the next move should restore a biblical view of human dignity, as the psalmist does in verses 5–8. The move could be heightened by an illustration from science about the extraordinarily precise conditions required of a universe capable of sustaining life. For example, renowned astrophysicist Martin Rees offers the following startling information about the size of our universe: "The very hugeness of our universe, which seems at first to signify how unimportant we are in the cosmic scheme, is actually entailed by our existence! This is not to say that there couldn't have been a smaller universe, only that we could not have existed in it."[11]

Other details about the fine tuning of our universe include the force of gravity, the tilt of the earth, the earth's near ideal positioning in orbit around just the right-sized star, the size of our universe, and the like. All of these could help to intensify the listeners' sense of wonder and awe at the majesty of God's wisdom and love as he called into being a world in which we are the crown and glory of his handiwork.

Because Psalm 8 has a special place in the New Testament—the author of Hebrews cites part of the psalm in reference to the person and work of Christ—we may wish to include a move in the sermon that deals with Christ's incarnation and atoning work. What stronger support is there for the degree of God's love for us than what we find in the central message of the gospel?

Psalm 8 in its original context does not make direct reference to Christ. However, the author of Hebrews clearly identifies Christ with the "son of man" of verse 4 in the psalm. Verse 2 of Psalm 8—which is somewhat difficult to interpret from the context of the rest of the psalm alone—introduces the topic of the enmity between God and humans. This opens the door to preaching on the incarnation and atonement without necessarily offering a full treatment of Hebrews 2 in the sermon.

If we wish to pair Psalm 8 with Hebrews 2, it might be advisable to preach two sermons. The first would comprise a full treatment of Psalm 8 as it functioned in its original context. The second sermon would focus more on Hebrews 2, but make major reference to Psalm 8.

The sermon suggestion offered here has several advantages. It remains faithful to the meaning embodied in the psalmist's words. It takes seriously the obstacles that ardent naturalistic scientists have attempted to erect against a theistic understanding of the cosmos. And it reassures those listeners who wonder how a God who is busy running such a huge universe could possibly care for them. If the cosmos were not the way it is, they could not be here to ask the question!

## Techniques for preserving a psalm's poetic effects

In conclusion, I would like to present a list of ten ways to maintain the poetic impact of the psalm as you develop your sermon.

1. Select a sermon structure similar to the psalm's structure in order to preserve some of the psalm's original rhetorical impact. (You may choose an entirely different structure for your sermon, but be aware of what effect your change will have on the psalm as it is filtered through the sermon.)

2. Decide whether to use an inductive or deductive sermon.

3. As a general rule, a sermon on a psalm should be arranged in moves (a series of developed ideas) rather than a traditional sermon outline structure of parallel points bridging from a single transition sentence in the introduction.

4. Build and release tension (if applicable) into your sermon in a way that mimics or respects the author's efforts to build and release tension.

5. Consider whether to help your listeners slow down and muse over one of the author's images, similes, metaphors, and the like. How will you develop key images in your sermon? Do you want to intensify some of their effects, keep them the same, or tone them down?

6. Select appropriate illustrations that work in concert with the rhetorical effects the psalmist achieved.

7. Select the mood of the sermon. Do you want to echo the author's mood?

8. Decide the point of view for the various moves of the sermon.

9. Use concrete, specific words in your sermon. Consider using parallelism as a way to restate your major ideas. For example: God loves sinners; sinners are the apple of God's eye.

10. Consider whether to pair the psalm with related Scriptures. For instance, should a sermon on Psalm 19 be linked with passages on the work of Christ?

For further reading on poetic analysis, see the notes.[12]

**Kenneth W. Smith** is minister of outreach and family ministry at First Baptist Church of Stoneham, Massachusetts.

# PART 2

# Sermon Application

# 7

# THE FUNDAMENTALS OF SERMON APPLICATION (PART 1)

*A step-by-step guide to getting application right.*

*Jeffrey Arthurs*

"Sermon application is like peeling an onion," says Haddon Robinson. "At first it seems easy, but as you go through layer after layer, all you have is tears." Robinson is right. The complex, interdisciplinary nature of homiletics shows its colors when we think about sermon application. Theology, hermeneutics, and exegesis are part of this art. For example, is Paul's injunction about women exercising authority still in force today, or was it limited to Timothy's setting? Sociology and psychology are part of application, because we must exegete the audience as well as the text. How does one preach Jesus as "master"—Greek *despotes*—to a democratic, pluralistic, and relativistic society? The preacher's own psyche comes into play as well. Some pastors shrink from application: "How dare we stand before our people claiming to be the arbiter of God's will? What hubris!"

Despite the difficulties, preachers know they must do application. They must do more than lecture about the Bible, because biblical truth is never divorced from life. David Larsen says, "A sermon which starts in the Bible and stays in the Bible is not biblical."[1]

In Carrell's study of ministers and congregations, *The Great American Sermon Survey*, application ranked first in pastors' own

> *[The preacher] is not to rest in general doctrine . . . [but should] bring it home by special use, by application to his hearers: which albeit prove a work of great difficulty to himself, requiring much prudence, zeal, and meditation . . . yet he is to endeavor to perform it in such a manner, that his auditors may feel the word of God to be quick and powerful, and a discerner of the thoughts and intents of the heart.*
> —Westminster Directory for the Publick Worship of God *(1645)*

description of why they preach. It also ranked first in listeners' desire for the sermon.[2] Listeners do not want to be marooned on the shores of abstraction. They want the truth brought into their zip code. Daniel Webster could have been part of the survey: "When a man preaches to me I want him to make it a personal matter, a personal matter, a personal matter."[3]

The question of application is quintessentially the preacher's question because the pastor more than any other is concerned with how the Bible intersects with real life and real people. For pastors, commissioned to feed God's sheep, the Bible is more than an academic or literary tome. It is bread for the hungry, milk for infants, a lamp for wanderers, and water for the stained. Those are the people who sit before us week in and week out.

But application is difficult, so in part 2 (chap. 8), I'd like to reduce the tears by presenting a four-stage process. Here in this chapter, let me define the term and sound a few cautions.

## What is application?

The term *application* comes from the Latin *ap* and *plico*, "to attach to or join," so that the one substance modifies another. We apply paint to a wall, pressure to a wound, and theory to practice. Application in a sermon takes the "theory" of the Word and brings it into contact with the listeners' hearts to produce change of behavior. Homileticians from previous eras used terms like *amplification, uses,* or *improvement,* but today's favored term is *application.* By the way, the term *improvement* did not imply that preachers made the text better, but that they use the text to make listeners better. That is the idea behind application.

> *The question of application is quintessentially the preacher's question because the pastor more than any other is concerned with how the Bible intersects with real life and real people.*

William Perkins, a Puritan divine, provides a definition of application that has stood the test of time: the "skill by which the doctrine which has been properly drawn from the Scriptures is handled in ways which are appropriate to the circumstances of the place and time and to the people in the congregation."[4]

Notice the following elements in the definition:

- Application is a "skill." This means that we can get better at it. That is why you're reading this material! To be sure, the ability to apply Scripture grows from spiritual gifts such as discernment, wisdom, teaching, and encouragement, but we can hone those gifts.

- Application assumes exegesis. In Perkins's definition, "Doctrine has been properly drawn from the Scriptures." Effective preachers work hard to "properly draw" the author's meaning. If we do not establish application on the rock of exegesis, we build on sand.

- Application assumes theology. Perkins's term is *doctrine*. The truths discovered in exegesis, framed in context-specific situations (such as slaves obeying masters), must be abstracted into theological and ethical principles before they can be reframed into the contemporary context. This reframing is the essence of application, which I develop here.

- Application demands audience analysis. It must be "appropriate" to the place, time, and people. This is why pastors who spend time with the flock, in contrast to itinerate preachers, are the most effective preachers. As Ian Pitt-Watson says, "Preaching divorced from pastoral concern is blind. It neither knows what it is talking about nor to whom it is talking."[5]

- Application includes explaining, persuading, motivating, and equipping. It is holistic, addressing the heart, not just behavior. Sometimes homileticians use the term *application* synonymously with urging behavioral change, but we should think of it more broadly than that. While the destination of sermon application is always behavior, the road winds through the back alleys of motivation or what the Bible calls the heart. The heart is the motivational structure out of which flow the issues of life. It is the great mass of the iceberg beneath the tip of visible behavior.

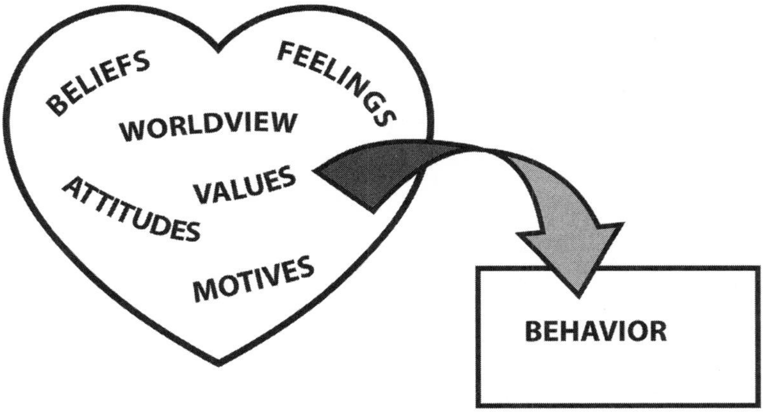


**Figure 7.1. Inner forces of the human heart affect behavior**

Maybe I'm stretching Perkins to fit my own view of application, but I don't think so. Perkins says that doctrine should be "handled in ways that are appropriate" to the particular listeners. Immature preachers often address only behavior (give more, pray more, do more, do better) without identifying and addressing the subterranean streams that percolate to the surface in behavior. Some people need information before they can act, so an "appropriate" ministry to them would be to educate or explain. Other people are skeptical, so we persuade. That is appropriate for them. Other people need to be motivated, and others need to be equipped. This holistic approach to sermon application saves us from triteness, because it helps us work toward *incremental* change by addressing the heart. People rarely change overnight. Exhorting people "never to complain again" won't work, but patient and careful exploration of the heart, which leads to less complaining, can be life changing. You see that application takes wisdom.

The best way to sanctify the heart, the way God uses most often in Scripture, is to display his magnificent character, especially his love and holiness. A vivid portrayal of God's overwhelming grace extended in Christ moves us to love him and serve what we love. That principle lies underneath the argumentation of the Epistles with their pattern of doctrine and then exhortation. (Incidentally, the Epistles are probably the best examples of what preaching to believers sounded like in the first century.) The argumentation goes like this: Husbands should love their wives *because* Christ loves the church (Eph. 5). Believers should give generously *because* Christ gave all (2 Cor. 8). As Randal Pelton states, "The first step of obedience is not, 'Do this,' but rather, 'Believe this and receive this.'"[6]

Argumentation based on theology is the best way to move the heart, but it is not the only way biblical authors persuade. They also appeal to our God-given desires for happiness ("Whoever desires to love life and see good days, let him keep his tongue from evil and his lips from speaking deceit" 1 Pet. 3:10 ESV), our desire to have our prayers answered ("Live with your wives in an understanding way . . . so that your prayers may not be hindered," 1 Pet. 3:7 ESV), and our inclination to imitate people we respect ("Brothers, join in imitating me" Phil. 3:17 ESV). For a larger catalog of biblically warranted motives, study the purpose clauses of the New Testament that begin with the Greek word *hina* ("so that"). Obey your parents *so that* you can have long life.

Obey God *so that* he will bless you. Give generously *so that* you will have treasure in heaven. When bathed in theology, such motives are not selfish or worldly. Preachers should promise all that God promises (not more than he promises) and warn of all that God warns of (not less).

The four components of application (explaining, persuading, motivating, and equipping) are psychologically sequential.[7] In Table 7.1 the upper components rest on the lower ones. An adult will not be *persuaded* of something she does not *understand*, because persuasion rests on explanation. If you were preaching on 1 Thessalonians 4:1–8, "Abstain from sexual immorality" (ESV), the components might look like those illustrated in Table 7.1 (see next page).

## How does application differ from interpretation?

Many evangelical writers distinguish between *meaning* and *significance*.[8] The first term is associated with interpretation and means the author's original intention, often summarized as a single proposition. The second is associated with application and means how the proposition might be relevant today. The dichotomy between meaning and significance helps us ground application in exegesis, because a text can never mean (significance) what it never meant (original meaning). The bridge-building metaphor of preaching assumes this dichotomy.

To take a well-worn example, "I can do all things through him [Christ] who strengthens me" (Phil. 4:13 ESV) does not mean (significance) that anyone who taps into the power of Christ can become rich, be healed from Alzheimer's, or win the state championship high jump. Paul did not have health and wealth in mind (original meaning). Rather, he was saying

**Table 7.1. Four Components of Application: 1 Thessalonians 4:1–8**

| | |
|---|---|
| **The Goal of Application for Listeners: Obedience/Action**<br>The listener abstains from sexual immorality. | **The Goal of Application for Preachers: Effective Ministry**<br>The preacher helps the listeners abstain from sexual immorality. |
| ↑<br>**Be Equipped**<br>"Okay, I feel the conviction of the Holy Spirit, and I want to change, but how?" | ↑<br>**Equip**<br>"Verse 6 says that no one should 'transgress and wrong his brother.' Here are some ways we can stop doing so." |
| ↑<br>**Feel Motivated**<br>"Okay, I agree that this is important to God, but there are other things that are important too—like keeping my boyfriend." | ↑<br>**Motivate**<br>"Verse 6 says that God is an 'avenger in all these things.' Such discipline looks like this." (Preacher gives examples and statistics of the problems associated with sexual immorality.) |
| ↑<br>**Agree**<br>"Okay, I understand what it means, but I don't think it is important to God." | ↑<br>**Persuade**<br>"It is important to God, as indicated in verse 3. Here is an analogy that helps us feel how important it is to God." |
| ↑<br>**Understand**<br>"What does 'sexual immorality' mean?" | ↑<br>**Explain**<br>"The term *porneia* means such and such, as illustrated by such and such." |
| **To obey, the listener needs to . . .** | **To help the listener obey, the preacher needs to . . .** |

that he could rejoice even while in trials. Christ gave him the strength to persevere and rejoice even in prison. Correct application does not yank words out of their context.

The dichotomy between meaning and significance keeps preachers from jumping too quickly to application before completely understanding the text, something we're apt to do since we want to help people live happy lives in Christ (not to mention that Sunday's a-comin', and we need something to say about our passage besides history and grammar!).

I appreciate the clarity of the dichotomy; however, as is true of many dichotomies, this one is simplistic. In real life, listeners do not distinguish between meaning and significance.[9] For them, the preacher's applications *are* the meaning of the text, and that view is similar to the one the New Testament authors had when they interpreted the Old Testament. Consider these verses that reveal Paul's hermeneutics, and notice that only a millimeter separates meaning and significance.

> For whatever was written in former days was written for our instruction, that through endurance and through the encouragement of the Scriptures we might have hope. (Rom. 15:4 ESV)

> But the words "it was counted to him" were not written for his sake alone, but for ours also. (Rom. 4:23–24 ESV)

> These things [incidents of Israel in the desert] happened to them as an example, but they were written for our instruction. (1 Cor. 10:11 ESV)

These three verses are not isolated examples. They represent the normal mind-set of biblical authors.[10] The dichotomy between meaning and significance is our concern not theirs, because they took a rhetorical perspective on the issue of meaning. That perspective broadens the traditional view of meaning to include not only ideational content but also function. From this perspective, utterances are not merely abstract repositories of concepts. Rather, they are an active force, the means an author uses to establish and modify a relationship with the person addressed. The use of words—a speech, sermon, epistle, poem, or story—is a speech act designed to *do* something. With words, the biblical authors, and behind them the divine Author, performed a catalog of actions from A to Z. They aroused, befriended, consoled, deterred, enlightened, fought, graced, honored, illumined, jeered. For the New Testament authors, meaning was not separated from significance. The Old Testament was alive and spoke to them. Or more exactly, God was alive, speaking to them through the Old Testament. Bernard Ramm captures the mind-set: "Holy Scripture is not a theoretical book of theological abstraction, but a book that intends to have a mighty influence on the lives of its readers."[11]

This discussion of meaning, authorial intention, and rhetoric is important for expository preachers because we yield to all the author intended—ideas *and* purpose. To make effective application, we discover the biblical author's rhetorical purpose (as well as his content) so that we can accomplish the same purpose in our sermons. Jay Adams describes this with the Greek term *telos* ("end, goal, purpose"),[12] a concept which will be crucial to my instruction in chapter 8, which lays out four stages for effective application. But to round off this chapter, let's talk about how *not* to do it. Many preachers are tripped by the following stumbling blocks.

## How *not* to do application

### 1. Undiscerning overemphasis on felt needs

This stumbling block sometimes lies on the road of seeker-targeted ministry with its passion for relevance. I applaud the passion, but too much emphasis on felt needs can cause a pastor to neglect the Bible. When felt needs are the preacher's primary concern, he or she starts with the audience, then scrambles around the pages of Scripture for verses that seem to address the topic, and ends up with an exegesis-thin, theology-lite sermon. The Bible doesn't say much about topics like retirement and putting the romance back into marriage.

> *In application we attempt to take what we believe is the truth of the eternal God, which was given in a particular time and place and situation, and apply it to people in the modern world who live in another time, another place, and a very different situation. That is harder than it appears.*
> —Haddon Robinson

The way to avoid this stumbling block is to dig beneath the surface of felt needs to discern God-given desires. Three of those desires are transcendence (the urge to count for something), security (the urge for protection), and community (the urge to belong). Effective preachers demonstrate that felt needs point to deeper needs and that the Bible offers shalom. As C. S. Lewis might say, effective preachers offer a holiday at the shore to children content with making mud pies in the slums.

## 2. Dogged commitment to the metanarrative

This stumbling block is sometimes found in the historical-redemptive camp, and it bears an unexpected resemblance to the previous one. Both neglect the text. If the first stumbling block comprises an overcommitment to the audience (if such a thing is possible), the second comprises an overcommitment to theology (if such a thing can be). Some historical-redemptive preachers drive so doggedly to the Cross that they neglect the distinctive features of particular texts. They sail along at thirty thousand feet pointing out the mountain peaks of the history of redemption, assuming that listeners make application themselves. This is not the biblical pattern.

While I am uncomfortable criticizing any sermon that drives to the Cross, I would point out that there is more theology in the Bible than the doctrine of redemption. The way to avoid this stumbling block is to let each text contribute its own strands to the tapestry of theology. Many of those strands will emphasize redemption, of course, but others might have the hues of creation, sanctification, or inspiration.

## 3. Unwarranted imagination

This is the stumbling block of allegorizing the text—turning the physical realities of biblical narratives into devotional analogies that do not align with the author's intention or the primary theology of the text. For example, a preacher could say that Elijah's pouring twelve casks of water on the altar shows that nothing can quench the fire of the Holy Spirit. The figurative use of Scripture is a subject of greater scope and complexity than I can deal with in detail here, for there are legitimate typological uses of Scripture. My purpose here is simply to say that imaginative excesses in application are a misuse of Scripture, and I encourage you to study further on the subject.

**4. Unintentional moralizing**

This stumbling block implies that we can earn God's grace by being good. While no Bible-believing preacher would say such a thing, we imply it regularly by our tone and emphases. With a laudable passion for personal holiness and human responsibility—both are biblical to the core—we may lead our listeners to conclude, I'd better be good or God won't like me.

Again, this is a topic too big to explore all the distinctions in this article. Church history testifies to the difficulty of getting law and grace, obedience and faith in proper relation to one another. Preachers of course do need to preach the whole counsel of God's will and how important it is that those saved by faith take it seriously. We cannot earn God's grace by being good, but we can fail to walk worthy of the gospel as authentic disciples and thus grieve the Lord and incur his fatherly rebuke. So the error of moralizing is once again often a matter of tone and emphasis, of failing to give proper preeminence to the grace and love of God.

The solution to this problem is to preach to the heart, wooing it with regular depictions of God's character, his grace in particular, while not neglecting reminders of God's holiness, discipline, and judgments. This is the model we see throughout the Bible. Yes, we preachers must hold believers accountable to high standards, but we help them live up to those standards by telling them over and over again of God's part in the covenant. He loves, calls, provides, sacrifices, protects, and enables us; therefore, we want to and are able to walk in covenant obedience, "to be good."

### 5. Simplistic *patternizing*

This is Daniel Overdorf's term for a stumbling block dug from the same quarry as moralizing. It turns descriptions of biblical characters into "universally normative prescriptions for behavior."[13] While the dogged devotee to the metanarratives is too reticent to apply details from stories, the simplistic patternizer is too quick to do so. Many biographical sermons exhort, "Be like David; don't be like Saul. Be like Moses; don't be like Miriam." Once again, I find some value in this approach, because providing examples was one reason biblical narrators told their stories. James sees a positive example in Elijah's "effectual fervent prayer" (James 5:16–17 KJV), and Peter sees a positive example in our Lord who did not revile when reviled (1 Pet. 2:21–23). Jesus himself, in the incident of the foot washing, left a normative prescription for behavior. He said, "I have given you an example, that you should do as I have done" (John 13:15 NKJV).

So the problem with the patternizing sermon is not that it does something the Bible does. Rather, it fails to do something *else* the Bible does. It fails to consider the authors' theological focus. They wrote primarily to tell us about God. The author of Ruth did not intend to give tips on how to get along with your in-laws. Neither did Mark record the story of the four fellows digging through the roof to model friendship evangelism. When preachers pursue their own purposes, rather than the *telos* of the author, they select only those details that help their case. A sermon titled "Lessons on Leadership from the Life of Moses" might sound like this: (1) pray, (2) walk with God, (3) delegate. But what about the other details of the narrative? I'd like to hear someone preach: (1) lose your temper, (2) murder, (3) marry someone outside the covenant. When patternizing sermons spin off of the Bible's theocentric axis, they are left with nothing but conventional wisdom.

So much for stumbling blocks. In the next chapter I'll present a four-stage process for building strong applications that combine audience relevance with biblical integrity.

**Jeffrey Arthurs** is the professor of preaching and communication, and the chair of the division of practical theology, at Gordon-Conwell Theological Seminary.

# 8

# THE FUNDAMENTALS OF SERMON APPLICATION (PART 2)

*A step-by-step guide to getting application right.*

*Jeffrey Arthurs*

In my previous chapter, I defined sermon application, broadening it to include more than simply exhorting good behavior or rebuking sin. While the goal of application is righteous living, the way to influence behavior is by addressing the heart, our motivational structure. Thus application includes explaining, proving, motivating, and equipping. The previous chapter also presented five stumbling blocks that trip preachers as they strive to be relevant.

Now it's time to present a biblically grounded, audience-sensitive approach to application. Figure 8.1 is a chart of the basic procedure. I'll illustrate each step with a sermon from Habakkuk titled "What to Do When Your Fig Tree Doesn't Blossom." To read the complete sermon, go to PreachingToday.com (http://www.preachingtoday.com/sermons/outlines/2011/november/figtreeblossom.html).

## How to apply with insight and accuracy

### Stage 1: discover the *telos* of the passage

By way of reminder, that Greek word *telos* refers to the author's rhetorical intention, his purpose. God intends his words to *do* things (Isa. 55:10–11; 2 Tim. 3:16). Thus Haddon Robinson says, "As part of your exegesis, you should ask, 'Why did the author write this? What effect did he expect it to have on his readers?' No biblical writer took up his pen to 'jot down a few thoughts' on religious subjects. Each one wrote to affect lives."[1] If that is true, then part of authorial intention is purpose, not just ideational content, and expository preachers want to be a conduit through whom God will fulfill his purpose.

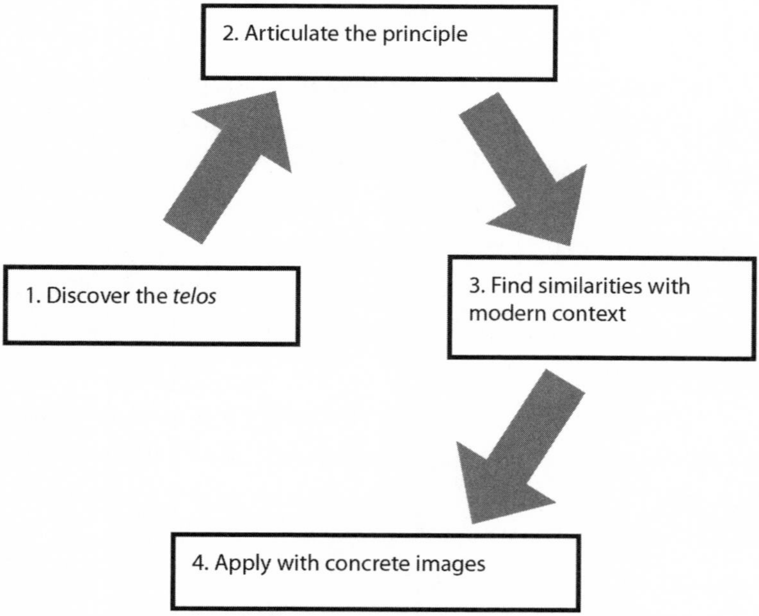


**Figure 8.1. Four stages of sermon application**

Of course this invites the question, how can I discover that purpose? Thankfully, sometimes the authors tell us what they hope to accomplish.

> These [things] are written so that you may believe. (John 20:31 NKJV)
>
> I felt the necessity to write to you urging you to contend earnestly for the faith. (Jude 3 NASB)
>
> . . . so that you may know how one ought to conduct himself in the household of God. (1 Tim. 3:15 NASB)

Most of the time, however, you need your best exegetical tools to discern purpose. While full discussion of that topic is beyond the scope of this teaching,[2] here is a short list of ways to exegete *telos*:

- **Notice authorial comment.** This is especially helpful with narrative, because that genre tends to "show" the truth rather than "tell" it plainly, but sometimes amid the showing the narrator inserts himself with comments like "The thing that David had done displeased the LORD" (2 Sam. 11:27 NKJV). Even parable, one of the most artistic and inductive genres, often begins or ends with a summary statement informing the reader of the *telos*. "To show them that they ought always to pray and not lose heart . . ." (Luke 18:1 ESV).
- **Explore the situation of the recipients.** Were they threatened with exile, under the chastising hand of God, so that they needed to repent? Had they been in exile for many years so that they needed to be encouraged that God was not done with them yet? Were they in danger

of drifting from Christ into the old practices of the first covenant? The more we know about the situation of the biblical readers, the better we can discern how God addressed that situation.

- **Explore the "fallen condition focus."**[3] This is Bryan Chapell's helpful concept. The FCF is linked to the point above, exploring the situation, but extends it with theological analysis. In light of the situation (such as exile), what problem linked to human fallenness did the biblical author seek to correct? The original audience may have needed encouragement, because they doubted the sovereignty or compassion of God. Or perhaps they needed a supportive community to help bear one another's burdens. The key is to understand how God corrected the fallen condition with his Word. Once you discern that, then you can find a similar circumstance your audience faces and address it the same way.

If you were preaching from Habakkuk, the first stage would look like that illustrated in Figure 8.2.

### Stage 2: articulate the principle(s)

Behind an author's *telos* for a particular situation and people lies a principle. The biblical author applied the principle in his concrete situation, and you will do the same in yours. Once you can articulate the principle, you are halfway home in sermon application. Some principles can be carried over without modification from the ancient text to the modern audience, such 1 Thessalonians 4:3, "Abstain from sexual immorality" (ESV). That principle will preach in any time and place, but more typically we will need to come up the ladder of abstraction.

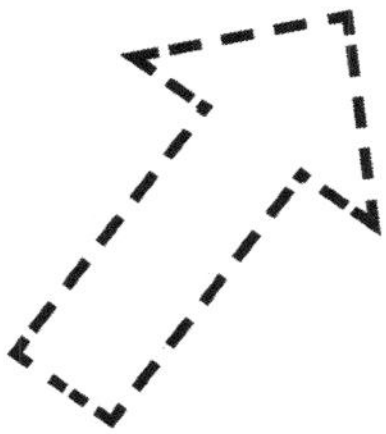

*Telos*
(Habukkuk's situation and God's purpose)

- Israel did not obey the Law.
- Habakkuk, representing the righteous people of Israel, lamented to God.
- God's answer, that the Chaldeans would ravage the land, confused Habakkuk even more.
- The FCF is fear, lack of understanding, and lack of trust in God.
- Thus, God helped Habakkuk to *live by faith*. That is the *telos* of the book.

**Figure 8.2. Application Stage 1: Habakkuk**

Remember Zipporah? God expressed his Word in a very concrete situation, a situation none of your listeners face, so you must climb the ladder to find the universal truth embedded in the concrete story. To say something timely from the story of Zipporah, you must first determine what is timeless.

Here's an example of the first two stages: the Corinthians were confused on the issue of financial support for ministers of the gospel, so the apostle Paul reached back into Deuteronomy. There the author of the Pentateuch laid down a law for an agrarian people: "Do not muzzle an ox while it is treading out the grain" (25:4). The fallen condition that made that law necessary was farmers' neglect or misuse of their animals. Digging deeper into the FCF: perhaps the ancient farmers had a mistaken view of their role as stewards of creation, so the lawgiver handed down God's injunction about oxen. Behind the specific injunction about oxen was a principle, and that principle applied not only to ancient Israel, but also to the Corinthians. Here is the principle: *the one who works at a task ought to share in its benefits.* Applied to the situation in Corinth, the principle means that "those who proclaim the gospel should get their living by the gospel" (1 Cor. 9:14 ESV). Jay Adams concludes: "The regulation concerning oxen was used to *exhibit* the principle; not to *limit* it."[4]

So far, using our example of Habakkuk, the stages look like the illustration of Figure 8.3.

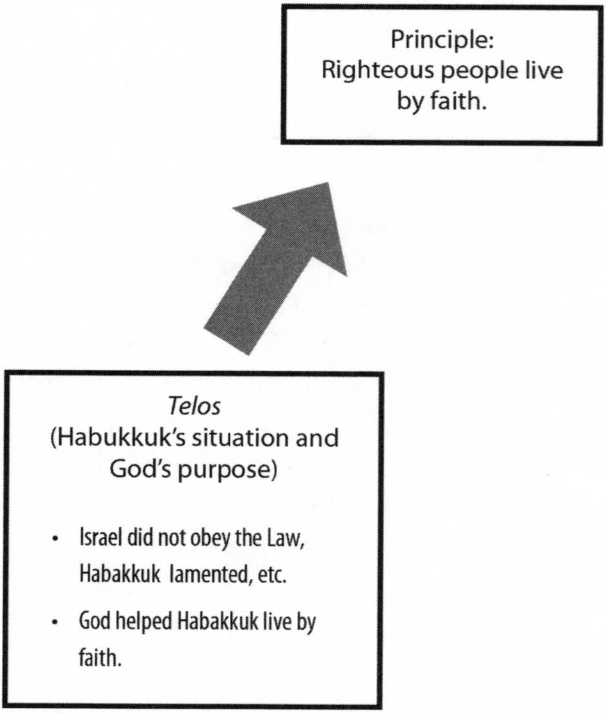
Principle:
Righteous people live
by faith.
*Telos*
(Habukkuk's situation and
God's purpose)
Israel did not obey the Law, Habakkuk lamented, etc.
God helped Habakkuk live by faith.

**Figure 8.3. Application Stages 1 and 2: Habakkuk**

### Stage 3: analyze your audience to find points of similarity

Having climbed the ladder of abstraction to articulate the principle(s), now climb down into the modern context to discern where your people face similar circumstances and how they are reacting to those circumstances. They are not facing invasion by the Chaldeans, but they *do* have their own troubles that cause them to lament at the ways of God.

Remember that effective application targets the heart, and to reach the heart we need to address the mind, the will, and the emotions. Thus sermon application includes explaining, proving, motivating, and equipping. Which of those do your people need in order to live by faith? What needs to happen to sanctify their hearts if you hope to see sanctified behavior? And remember that the best way to bring about change of heart is by pointing to the grace of God. Consider Tim Keller's approach:

> If I had preached on lying ten years ago, I might have said, "Don't lie. Tell the truth because Jesus is truth. And if you have lied, Jesus will forgive you." That appeal stops at changing external behavior. Today I might preach: "Let me tell you why you're not going to be a truthful person. I lie most often to avoid others' disapproval. If I just try to stop lying, it won't work because my need for others' approval overwhelms my good intentions. I allow other people, instead of Jesus, to determine my worth. If you want to stop lying, you have to find what is motivating your sin—like my

> *Effective application targets the heart, and to reach the heart we need to address the mind, the will, and the emotions.*

tendency to look to others for affirmation—and replace it with the security you can find in Jesus."[5]

Returning to Habakkuk, many listeners will need *information*. (Who were the Chaldeans? What was going on? What does it mean to live by faith?) Many will also need *proof.* (You tell me to trust God, but he doesn't seem trustworthy; you seem to be saying that faith is a magic wand that will cure all my problems, but that doesn't ring true.) The third component, *motivation,* will not play a major role in this sermon, but the last component will. The listeners will need concrete action steps that *equip* them to live by faith. In my sermon on Habakkuk, I exhorted the listeners with this action step: "repeat and remember." That is what Habakkuk did, and it enabled him to rejoice even as he waited for the awful day of invasion. I developed the general exhortation, "repeat and remember," with specific suggestions on how to do so: remember God's faithfulness when you take Communion; surround yourself with friends who will remind you of God's trustworthy character; and so forth.

You may be wondering how to discern the listeners' response to the principle you have discovered in your exegesis. This is where audience analysis comes in. Here are some ways to "exegete" the congregation. You don't need to do all of these for every sermon, but you should do some of them for each sermon and all of them from time to time.

- **Start with yourself.** What do *you* not understand, believe, or obey? Why do you lack motivation to follow the principle? What is keeping you back? While your issues are not identical to the issues of the "man in the pew," there is a great deal of overlap. Furthermore, even if you do not use overt self-disclosure in the sermon, exegeting yourself adds a tone of authenticity and humility that will pervade the sermon in subtle ways.

- **Informal contact.** This the fundamental source of information for audience analysis. When pastors work with, play with, and pray with their sheep, they come to know them by name. When you are with your people, there is no need to pump them to discover their views on every subject. Just "hang out" with them.

- **Counseling.** While we never reveal confidential matters in the pulpit, we pay attention to trends, lifestyles, and worldviews prevalent among our people.

- **Empathetic imagination.** This is Fred Craddock's phrase.[6] A few times a year write this question on the top of a blank sheet of paper: What is it like to. . . ? Then choose a concrete circumstance. What is it like to be homeless? To be a benchwarmer? To have inherited a small fortune? Then spend fifteen minutes writing down every thought, image, memory, or experience you can think of. While you may have never inherited a small fortune, you probably have enough vicarious experience to make an educated guess at what it's like. Craddock says that those fifteen minutes will give you a wealth of illustrative material and add empathy to your sermons.

- Open your church's **pictorial directory** and "listen" to the principle ("Righteous people live by faith") through the ears of Mrs. Smith, who is recently remarried, Juan the barber, Jill the cheerleader, or Bobby with his broken wrist. What do you need to explain or prove? Do you need to inspire or equip? Alternatively, instead of using the church directory, just use your imagination as you subject the principle to segments of your congregation—the skeptics or the teenagers who slouch in the last row.

- Create a **feed-forward group.** In addition to getting feed*back*, try seeking input before you preach. This is becoming increasingly common among North American pastors. Some create focus groups to get input on a topic that is coming up on the preaching calendar. Other pastors use a standing group such as the church staff, elders, or local preachers.
- **Survey the congregation** with a tool like Willow Creek's *Reveal*. My church used that instrument, and I was shocked to learn that less than half of the attendees believed in the inerrancy of the Bible. That knowledge prompted me to beef up my persuasion. I could not assume that people were buying my statements just because they were in the Bible.
- **Pay attention to culture.** This is the most general type of audience analysis, but it also is necessary. What does culture laugh at? Who are its heroes? What are its god-terms?

Stage 3 looks like the illustration in Figure 8.4.

### Stage 4: apply (that is, explain, prove, motivate, and equip) with concrete images

To *explain* the meaning of faith, a story, example, or analogy is better than a dictionary definition. To *prove* that faith really

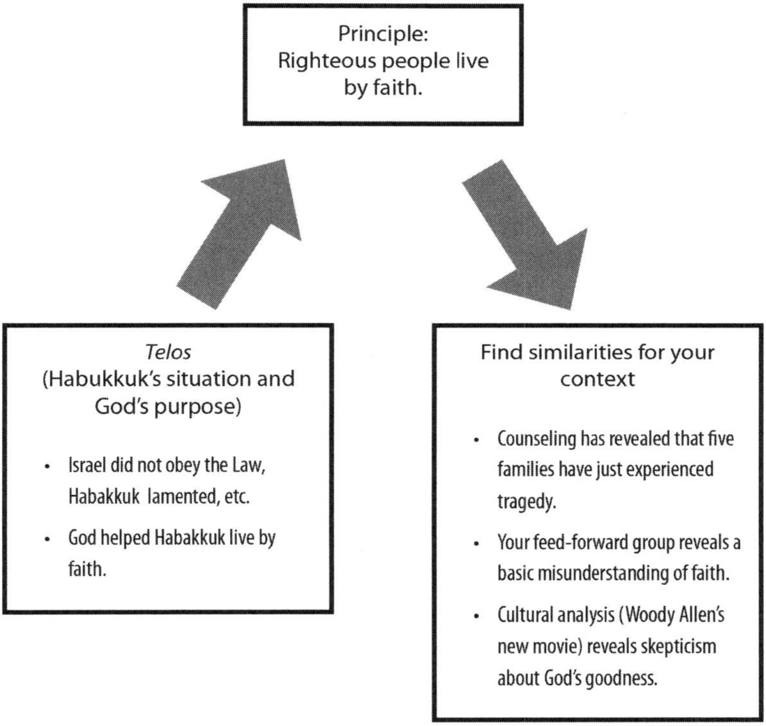
Principle:
Righteous people live by faith.
Telos
(Habukkuk's situation and God's purpose)
Israel did not obey the Law, Habakkuk lamented, etc.
God helped Habakkuk live by faith.
Find similarities for your context
Counseling has revealed that five families have just experienced tragedy.
Your feed-forward group reveals a basic misunderstanding of faith.
Cultural analysis (Woody Allen's new movie) reveals skepticism about God's goodness.

**Figure 8.4. Application Stage 3: Habakkuk**

does help us rejoice in the midst of trials, a testimony is better than a syllogism. To *motivate*, nothing beats self-disclosure. Reveal your heart and let the people know how the principle is impacting you. As Bill Hybels says, "The speed of the leader is the speed of the team." To *equip*, suggest concrete action steps of how to live by faith. The human mind is a picture gallery, not a debating chamber.

Bryan Chapell calls stage 4 "situational specificity."[7] Which parishioner, upon settling into his or her seat, does not know that we are supposed to love our neighbors? Merely trumpeting that biblical principle adds little to the listener's spiritual maturity, but the word takes wing when we talk about loving the neighbor who belongs to a different political party, whose front yard is a trash heap, or who backs into your car but does not leave a note. The aptness and concreteness of situational specificity is a mark of mature preaching.

> *The common people are captivated more readily by comparisons and examples than by difficult and subtle disputations. They would rather see a well-drawn picture than a well-written book.*
> —Martin Luther

The use of situational specificity is especially crucial in the introduction. When we start with life as the listeners actually live it, we immediately gain attention and surface need. Take some advice from the editor of the *Brooklyn Eagle,* H. V. Kaltenborn: "Always remember that a dog fight in Brooklyn is more important than a revolution in China."[8] Let the first words out of your mouth "promise" the listeners that the next thirty minutes are going to be a word from God to them, for them, and about them.

Stage 4 is illustrated in Figure 8.5.

Application may be the hardest part of preaching, but when "the flint of someone's problem strikes the steel of the Word of God, a spark emerges that can set that person on fire for God."[9]

For further suggested reading, see the notes.[10]

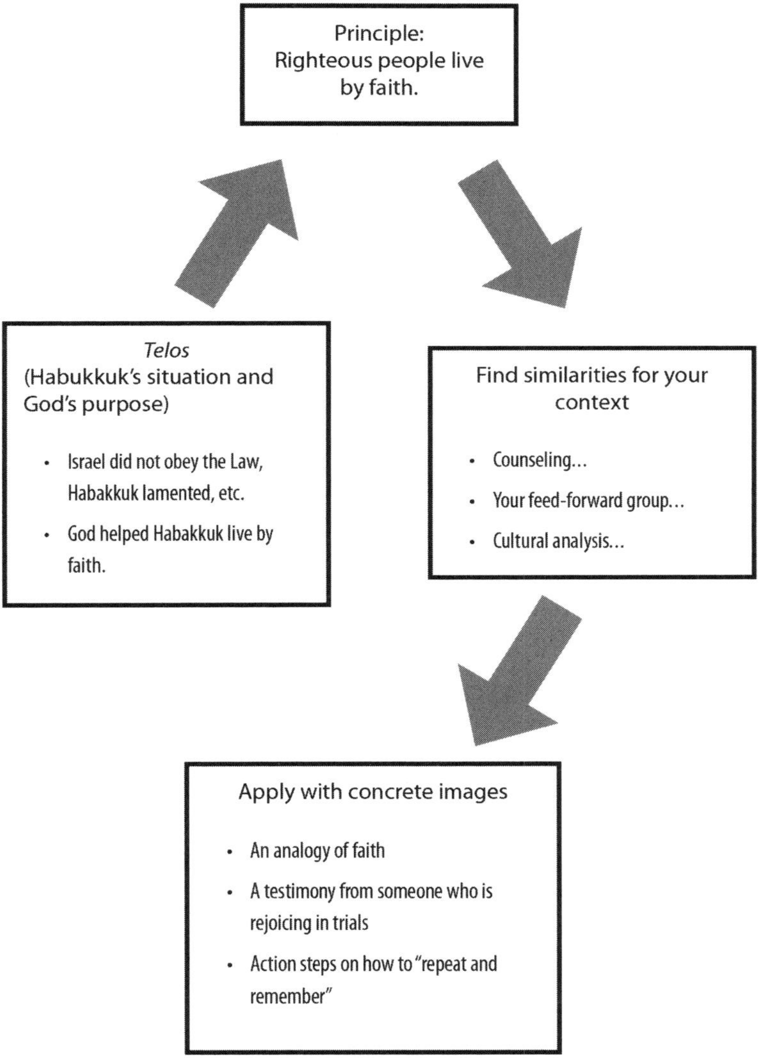
Principle:
Righteous people live
by faith.
*Telos*
(Habukkuk's situation and
God's purpose)
• Israel did not obey the Law, Habakkuk lamented, etc.
• God helped Habakkuk live by faith.
Find similarities for your
context
• Counseling...
• Your feed-forward group...
• Cultural analysis...
Apply with concrete images
• An analogy of faith
• A testimony from someone who is rejoicing in trials
• Action steps on how to "repeat and remember"

**Figure 8.5. Application Stage 4: Habakkuk**

**Jeffrey Arthurs** is the professor of preaching and communication, and the chair of the division of practical theology, at Gordon-Conwell Theological Seminary.

9

# BLENDING BIBLE CONTENT AND LIFE APPLICATION

*Sound advice on four practical issues of sermon application.*

*Haddon Robinson*

It was a disastrous sermon. A church in Dallas invited me to preach on John 14. That's not an easy passage. It is filled with exegetical questions about death and the Second Coming. How do you explain, "If I go and prepare a place for you, I will come again, and receive you unto myself" (KJV)? How is Jesus preparing that place? Does Jesus mean we won't go to be with him until he comes back? What about soul sleep? I spent most of my week studying the text and reading the commentaries to answer questions like these.

When I got up to preach, I knew I had done my homework. Though the issues were tough, I had worked through them and was confident I was ready to deliver solid biblical teaching on the assigned passage.

Five minutes into the sermon, though, I knew I was in trouble. The people weren't with me. At the ten-minute mark, people were falling asleep. One man sitting near the front began to snore. Worse, he didn't disturb anyone! No one was listening.

Even today, whenever I talk about that morning, I still get an awful feeling in the pit of my stomach.

What went wrong? The problem was that I spent the whole sermon wrestling with the tough theological issues, issues that intrigued me. Everything I said was valid. It might have been strong stuff in a seminary classroom. But in that church, in that pulpit, it was a disaster.

What happened? I didn't speak to the life questions of my audience. I answered my questions, not theirs. Some of the men and women I spoke to that day were close to going home to be with the Lord. What they wanted to know was "Will he toss me into some ditch of a grave, or will he take me safely home to the other side? When I get to heaven, what's there?"

They wanted to hear me say, "You know, Jesus said he was going to prepare a place for us. The Creator of the universe has been spending two thousand years preparing a home for you. God only spent six days creating the world, and look at its beauty! Imagine, then, what the home he has been preparing for you must be like. When you come to the end of this life, that's what he'll have waiting for you."

That's what I should have preached. At least I should have started with their questions. But I didn't.

It's also possible to make the opposite error—to spend a whole sermon making practical applications without rooting them in Scripture. I don't want to minimize Scripture. It's possible to preach a skyscraper sermon—one story after another with nothing in between. Such sermons hold people's interest but give them no sense of the eternal. Talking about "mansions over the hilltop" comes from country-western music, not the

Bible. A sermon full of nonbiblical speculations is ultimately unsatisfying.

Some of the work I did in my study, then, could have helped the people answer their questions. The job is to combine both biblical content and life application in an effective way.

## How much content is enough?

How then can we strike the right balance in our preaching between biblical content and life application?

The basic principle is to give as much biblical information as the people need to understand the passage, and no more. Then move on to your application.

The distinction between exegesis and exposition is helpful here. Exegesis is the process of getting meaning from the text, often through noting the verb tense or where the word emphasis falls in the original languages. That's what you do in your study as you prepare. But it's seldom appropriate in a sermon on Sunday morning. In fact, an overuse of Greek or Hebrew can make us snobs. Using the jargon of my profession can come across as a putdown, a way of saying, I know something you don't know. There's an arrogance about that that can create distance between me and the audience.

I served for ten years as a general director of the Christian Medical and Dental Society. Sometimes physicians would use technical medical terms when they talked with me, and I wouldn't know what they were talking about. Once I said to one of my friends, "I hope you don't talk to your patients as you do to me, because I don't know the jargon. I'm an educated person. I just don't happen to be as educated in medicine as you are."

Do you know what he said to me? He replied, "Preachers do that in the pulpit all the time."

I did a lot of that when I first got out of seminary. I used my knowledge of Greek and Hebrew in the study and in the pulpit. One day a woman wounded me with a compliment: "I just love to hear you preach. In fact, when I see the insights you get from the original languages, I realize that my English Bible is hardly worth reading."

I went home asking myself, "What have I done? I'm trying to get people into their Bibles, but I've taken this lady out of hers."

Spurgeon was right: the people in the marketplace cannot learn the language of the academy, so the people in the academy must learn the language of the marketplace. It's the pastor's job to translate.

While raw exegesis doesn't belong in a Sunday morning sermon, what does belong there is exposition. Exposition is drawing from your exegesis to give the people what they need to understand the passage. They don't need all you've done in exegesis, but they do need to see the framework, the flow of the passage. They should be able to come back to the passage a few weeks after you've preached on it, read it, and say, "Oh, I understand what it says."

Does this mean there is no place in the church for exegesis? Of course not. As you study, you may dig out all kinds of material that would help certain people who enjoy detailed Bible study. While including these tidbits in a sermon resembles distracting footnotes, this kind of technical teaching is appropriate for a classroom.

Some pastors I know preach on a passage on Sunday and then follow up with a detailed exegetical study with a smaller group of interested people on Wednesday night.

Donald Gray Barnhouse had an interesting way of handling this. He commented as he did the Scripture reading. He would pause as he read to talk briefly about the tense of a verb or what some expression meant. He'd take ten minutes just reading the Scripture. His Bible reading was based on his exegesis.

Even then, Barnhouse did not show off. He didn't give his congregation lessons in ancient languages. He simply took time to amplify the passage based on his study so that his people could appreciate the flow and nuances of the thought of the biblical writer. Some folks attending Tenth Presbyterian Church for the first time heard the Bible reading and thought they had heard the sermon!

When Barnhouse got to his sermon, he was able to concentrate on the message of that passage, its implications, its application, which is what makes a sermon a sermon.

## The "so what?" of preaching

All preaching involves a "so what?" A lecture on the archaeology of Egypt, as interesting as it might be, isn't a sermon. A sermon touches life. It demands practical application.

That practical application, though, need not always be spelled out. Imagine, for example, that you borrow my car, and it has a flat. You call me up and say, "I've never changed a tire on a car like this. What do I do?"

I tell you how to find the spare, how to use the jack, where to find the key that unlocks the wire rim. Once I give you all the instructions, then do I say, "Now, I exhort you: change the tire"? No, you already want to get the car going. Because you already sense the need, you don't need exhortation. You simply need a clear explanation.

Some sermons are like that. Your people are wrestling with a certain passage of Scripture. They want to know what it means. Unless they understand the text, it's useless to apply it. They don't need exhortation; they need explanation. Their questions about the text must be answered.

You may not need to spell out practical application when you are dealing with basic theological issues—how we see God and ourselves and each other. For example, you might preach on Genesis 1, showing that it's not addressing issues of science so much as questions of theology: what is God like? You might spend time looking at the three groups of days—the first day is light, the fourth day is lights; the second day is sea and sky, the fifth day is fish and birds. Each day is followed by God's evaluation: "It was good." But after the creation of man, God observes, "It was very good."

Then you ask, "What do we learn about God?" We learn that God is good, that God has a purpose in creation. We learn that while every other living thing is made "after its own kind," man and woman are created in God's image. What does that say about people—the people we pray with and play with, the people we work with or who sleep on the streets?

The whole sermon may be an explanation with little direct application built into it. Of course, that doesn't mean there's no application. If at the close of this sermon someone realizes, "That's a significant statement about who we are. There are no ordinary people. Every man and woman has special worth"—when that really sinks in—it can make tremendous practical differences as it shapes how a person sees himself and other people.

Or take Romans 3. You might begin by raising in some practical way the question, how does a person stand right before God? Then you could lead your listeners through Paul's rather complex discussion of what it means to be justified by faith. If you do it well, when you are finished, people should say, "So that's how God remains righteous when he declares us righteous."

Obviously, this passage has great application. But it's so complex you probably couldn't go through Paul's argument and spell out in any detail many practical applications, too, in the same sermon. And that's okay. If they really understood the problem of lostness, the solution of salvation serves as a strong application.

We need to trust people to make some of their own practical applications. Some of the best growing I've done has taken place when a concept gripped me, and I found myself constantly thinking, "How could this apply in my life?"

Of course, you do have knowledge your people don't possess, knowledge they expect you to have and share with them. But you can share that knowledge in a manner that doesn't talk down to a congregation, in a way that says, "If you were in my situation, you'd have access to the same information." If you feel you must make all the practical applications for your hearers, do their thinking for them, you underestimate their intelligence. You can dishonor your congregation if you tell them in effect, "You folks couldn't have figured out for yourselves how this applies."

For me, though, the greater danger lies in the opposite direction—in spending too much time on explanation and not going far enough into application. After preaching I've often come away feeling, "I should have shown them in a more specific way how to do this." It is difficult for our listeners to live by what they believe unless we answer the question, how?

## Real-life examples: necessary but dangerous

To make a principle come to life—to show how it can be applied—we need to give specific real-life examples, illustrations that say, here is how someone faced this problem, and this is what happened with her. But as necessary as real-life examples are, they carry a danger.

Suppose, for example, that someone preaches on the principle of modesty. Should a Christian dress with modesty? The answer is yes. But how do you apply that? One preacher may say, "Well, any skirt that's above the knee is immodest." So he ends up with a church full of knee-length people. In that church, one application of a principle has assumed all the force of the principle itself. That is the essence of legalism: giving to a specific application the force of the principle.

I have a friend who keeps a journal, and it works for him. But when he preaches about it, he makes it sound as though Christians who are not journaling can't be growing. Whenever you say, "If you're not doing this particular act, then you're not following this principle," that's legalism.

How, then, can you preach for practical application if every time you say, "This is how to apply this truth," you run the risk of promoting legalism? Let me answer with a couple of examples.

When my father was in his eighties, he came to live with us. After a while he grew senile, and his behavior became such that we could no longer keep him in our home. Because his erratic behavior endangered himself and our children, we had to put him in a nursing home. It cost me half my salary each month to keep him there. For eight years, until he died, I visited my dad almost every day. In eight years I never left that rest home without feeling somewhat guilty about his being there. I would have preferred to have had him in our home, but we could not care for him properly.

A few years later, my mother-in-law, who was dying of cancer, came to live with us in our home in Denver. It was a tough period in our marriage. I was trying to get settled as president of Denver Seminary. My wife, Bonnie, was up with her mother day and night. She somehow changed her mother's soiled bed six or seven times a day. For eighteen months Bonnie took care of her in our home. When Mrs. Vick died, we had no regrets. We knew Bonnie had done everything she could to make her last months comfortable.

How should Christians care for their aging parents? Do you keep them in your home, or do you place them in a nursing facility? There is no single Christian answer. It depends on your situation, your children, your resources, and your parents.

There is, though, a single guiding principle: we must honor our parents and act in love toward them. To make a Christian decision, you can't start with a selfish premise; you start by asking what is best for everyone involved. How you apply that principle in a given situation depends on a complex set of variables.

The way to avoid the trap of legalism, then, is to distinguish clearly between the biblical principle and its specific applications. One way to do this in preaching is to illustrate a principle with two or three varying examples, not just one, so you don't equate the principle with one particular way of applying it.

When our children were young, I lived under the idea that if we didn't have daily devotions with our children—a family altar—somehow we were failing God. The problem was, family devotions worked for other people, but although we tried all kinds of approaches, they never worked for us. Our children sat still for them on the outside but ran away from them on the inside. Yet we kept at them, because I felt that a family altar was at the heart of a Christian family.

Then I realized that family devotions wasn't the principle, but the application of a principle. The principle was that I needed to bring up my children to know and love God. I had mistakenly been giving to our family devotions the same imperative that belonged to the principle behind it.

We then came up with a different approach, one that worked for us. Our two children left for school at different times. Each morning before Vicki left, I would pray with her about the day, about what was coming up. A little later Torrey and one of his friends came into my study, and we'd sit and pray for five minutes about what their day held.

That may not sound as satisfying in a sermon as saying we had devotions as a family at the breakfast table every morning, but for us it was an effective way to honor the principle. A preacher must make a clear distinction between the principle and its applications.

This is not to say, however, that a biblical principle must sound abstract and vague. Sometimes a preacher merely translates the principle into terms that a congregation understands.

In our American frontier days, there was a settlement in the west whose citizens were engaged in the lumber business. The town felt they wanted a church. They built a building and called a minister. The preacher moved into the settlement and initially was well received. Then one afternoon he happened to see some of his parishioners dragging some logs, which had been floated down the river from another village upstream, onto the bank. Each log was marked with the owner's stamp on one end. To his great distress, the minister saw his members pulling in the logs and sawing off the end where the telltale stamp appeared. The following Sunday he preached a strong sermon on the commandment "Thou shalt not steal." At the close of the service, his people lined up and offered enthusiastic congratulations. "Wonderful message, Pastor. Mighty fine preaching." The response bothered him a great deal. So he went home to prepare his sermon for the following Sunday. He preached the same sermon but gave it a different ending: "And thou shalt not cut off the end of thy neighbor's logs." When he got through, the congregation ran him out of town.

It's possible to state the principle in terms the audience clearly understands.

## "We" preaching and "you" preaching

Another way to view the relationship between explanation and application is to look at the pronouns each calls for. Good preachers identify with their hearers when they preach. All of *us* stand before God to hear what God's Word says to *us*. The Letter to the Hebrews says that the high priest was taken from among men to minister in the things pertaining to man. The high priest knew what it was to sin and to need forgiveness. With the people, he stood before God in need of cleansing. In identifying with the people, he represented the people to God.

But that same priest, by offering a sacrifice, could minister God's cleansing to the people. Not only did he represent the people to God, he also represented God to the people. Somehow, that's also what preaching does.

When I'm listening to a good sermon, there comes a point when I lose track of all the people around me. As the preacher speaks, I experience God talking to me about me. The time for explanation has passed; the time for application has come.

At that point, it's appropriate for the preacher to leave behind "we" in favor of "you." No longer is the preacher representing the people to God; he is representing God to the people. "We've seen the biblical principle; we've seen two or three ways others have applied it. Now what does this say to you?"

*Life-changing preaching does not talk to the people about the Bible. Instead, it talks to the people about themselves—their questions, hurts, fears, and struggles—from the Bible.*

"You've got to decide how you're going to spend your money."

"You've got to decide whether you're going to take your marriage vows seriously."

It's you—not *you* plural, but *you* singular—you personally who must decide what you will do with the truth you've heard.

For the preacher to say "you" at that point isn't arrogant; he's not standing apart from the congregation. He's simply challenging each listener to make personal application.

In the final analysis, effective application does not rely on techniques. It is more a stance than a method. Life-changing preaching does not talk to the people about the Bible. Instead, it talks to the people about themselves—their questions, hurts, fears, and struggles—from the Bible. When we approach the sermon with that philosophy, flint strikes steel. The flint of someone's problem strikes the steel of the Word of God, and a spark emerges that can set that person on fire for God.[1]

**Haddon Robinson** is Harold John Ockenga Distinguished Professor of Preaching at Gordon-Conwell Theological Seminary. He is author of *Biblical Preaching* (Baker).

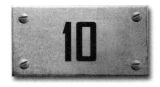

# 10

# THE PLACE OF PASTORAL WISDOM IN APPLICATION

*To what extent should sermon application be guided by personal experience, observation, and common sense?*

*Timothy S. Warren*

*If we pay extremely close attention to the source of authority for what we say in a sermon, we might be surprised at how often our statements of application are not based directly on Scripture. In this interview Timothy Warren of Dallas Theological Seminary discusses what we should think of this common practice.*

**In a conversation you and I had in the past about sermon application, you used the phrase *pastoral wisdom preaching*, which caught my attention. What do you mean by that?**

I tell my kids, "Don't play in the street." That's not based on a text, but it is based on my wisdom and experience. Sometimes we tell our people things that are not necessarily based on a text but are good common sense. Leave the visitors the close parking spaces. If you see somebody who looks confused walking in the door of the church, go up and introduce yourself. Be friendly and invite them in. I could find a text to make that work, but that's common sense. So pastoral wisdom preaching happens all the time. The question is, to what extent can that happen in a sermon?

I believe we can preach with some significant level of authority an application that is not explicitly mentioned in the text. The question is not, do I do it with any authority? but rather, with what level of authority, or what authority am I drawing on? Am I drawing on simply my own ethos and experience? Or am I drawing on biblical authority? That's where we have to be clear when it comes to applicational statements.

Expository preaching is not limited simply to preaching through the text; we can preach the idea of the text. It's the theological message. The question is, how do I supply that principle? How do I apply that indicative statement about who God is and how I relate to him? The application is the responsibility of the preacher, unless the text is explicit about it. In the Epistles it is more explicit. In a lot of the other literature, it isn't explicit. So we're either going to leave sermon application at an exegetical level or in theological abstraction at a principle level, or we're going to take responsibility to speak out of our wisdom. That's where we are asking, how do we move from a textually derived theological idea, proposition, concept, theme? And where do we go from there?

To move from that established theological concept to application, if we don't have a direct correlation, as we do in the Epistles, we need to build some bridges for the audience. Sometimes we build psychological bridges; we build sociological bridges; we build logical bridges; we build traditional bridges. We do this by saying, "It makes sense that if this is true, then this would be an application."

**Let's look at 2 Corinthians 6 as an example.**

"Do not be yoked together with unbelievers" (2 Cor. 6:14). When you look at the context, Paul is saying, I want you to pay attention to me. I wrote these things to you because I saw a danger. Don't be unequally yoked together.

He is alluding to Deuteronomy 22:10, which says, "Do not plow with an ox and a donkey yoked together." You have to go back to that and show that God was teaching the whole concept of separation. "Don't wear wool and linen together. You can eat oxen, but you can't eat shrimp." God was teaching a theology of separation. Paul is saying, I'm teaching you a theology of separation. You cannot be Christian and still dabble in the behavior of your pagan community like you used to. You cannot be Christian and give in to the false teaching threatening the church. I'm calling on you not to have communion, fellowship, partnership, or harmony with unbelievers, because it's not natural. You're the temple of God.

You've got to do all of that exegetical and theological work before you have any credibility in making application. I've primarily heard the application of "don't be unequally yoked together" as related to marriage. That's a legitimate application. That's not Paul's application. Paul's application is don't put yourself in a mismatched spiritual relationship with the pagans and behave as they behave. Don't put yourself in a mismatched spiritual relationship with false teachers. So it wasn't marriage here; it was friendships, relationships.

It probably does have application to marriage. That's not what the text is saying. Given what the text says and the theology behind it, related to Israel not intermarrying with the Canaanites and learning the principle of separation, how do I apply that today? To make it relevant to marriage, I have to show the connection. When you marry somebody, you become involved in an intimate, whole-person relationship. You cannot be married to somebody and not have your spiritual worldview, your faith, influenced. There's a legitimate application here based on wisdom, based on logic, based on how people relate to each other in communication. I can build that bridge. I could apply that with a high level of authority, because I can build a firm platform for hearers to follow.

How about business partnerships? There are some business partnerships you could be involved in with unbelievers because the nature of the businesses and the particular moral position these partners have, even though they may not be believers, is not going to involve you in spiritual compromise. There are other business relationships where you couldn't be involved with an unbeliever, because the relationship has too much spiritual input. The whole integrity of the business is going to keep you from being able to do whatever it is.

For example, if you own a convenience store, you decide what you're going to sell. Are you going to sell cigarettes? Are you going to sell beer? Are you going to sell lottery tickets? Are you going to sell condoms? How am I going to be in relationship with somebody who doesn't share my spiritual values when we're deciding what to sell?

I would apply that passage about an unequal yoke with a lot more tentativeness to a business relationship than I would to a marriage. If I preached that passage, and I said to my people, "This definitely means you should not marry an unbeliever. It possibly means you should not go into business with some people. It requires discernment, just as it required discernment for ancient Israel. God was teaching them this lesson of separation when he said what you can or can't eat, what you can or can't wear, and that you shouldn't put an ox and a donkey together." There would be some tentativeness. I would say to my congregation, "I am certain a marriage yoke would violate the theological principle of discerning separation from badly matched spiritual relationships. I encourage you to evaluate any business relationship you might get into, because that partnership may or may not lead you into a position of compromise."

**Would you say we have been looking at basically two categories of authority—the definite or the maybe?**

Ramesh Richard wrote a series of articles in *Bibliotheca Sacra* about application. He said within certain texts there are statements we can directly apply. "Thou shalt not commit adultery." There are other passages we can draw implications out of, and there are still other passages that the best we can do is extrapolate.

With "Thou shalt not commit adultery," the *direct application* is easy. Don't commit adultery. An *implication* of that would be the sanctity of marriage. In other words, work on your marriage; that's a legitimate application of the passage. Work on your marriage to make sure it's fulfilling and you don't wander physically or emotionally or spiritually. If I were to make the application, "Never go out to a lunch or dinner with a person of the opposite sex alone," that would be an *extrapolation*. It may be wisdom. It may be a good policy. But it isn't an absolute. It would probably be wise not to be in a setting where you could easily compromise yourself or your reputation.

**Suppose you are presenting a message that gives biblical advice about what to do after you've been divorced. What kind of guardrails do we need to keep on the application?**

There is a place for the pastor, even on Sunday morning, to stand up and say, "I'm not going to preach a sermon. I'm going to address an issue many of you face—the issue of how to go on from here after a divorce. I don't even have a text today, but I just want to share with you some things I think are going to be helpful to you." I wouldn't have a problem with doing that. I'd have more of a problem with saying, "My text today is—" and then stretching the text to make it cover my topic.

There's a place to say to a congregation, "I'm just going to share some wisdom. It's biblical wisdom, but from a lot of texts. It's orthodox. I think it's wise. But I'm not saying it is 'thus saith the Lord.' This is from my years of counseling and experience."

Take 1 Timothy 4:16, for example. Paul tells Timothy, "Give attention to yourself" (NET). Paul had just talked about not letting people look down on his youth. Be an example in love, faith, and purity. When he says, "Give attention to yourself," the idea is, give attention to your doctrine and to your godly behavior.

Someone could use that text to springboard into how a pastor needs to give attention to himself so he can have credibility—things like how he dresses, grooms himself, polishes his shoes, or washes his car before he drives to the church on Sunday morning—all of those things may be good advice out of the experience of the pastor. They probably have a place in a seminary chapel setting for people who are preparing for ministry. But you don't need a text for that. To choose a text makes it appear that you're saying, since I have a text, this is what God is saying to you today. It gives the advice the same level of authority or ethos as the instructions "Don't commit adultery"; "walk in the way of the law of the Lord"; "trust Jesus by faith, not works, for salvation." We call into question our own integrity when we don't acknowledge the source of the authority for what we are saying. Sometimes it's just me, the preacher, or me, the dad.

I tell my kids, "There are a lot of things I won't go to the wall on, but let me tell you the things I will go to the wall on. They're in the Bible, and I can give you chapter and verse, in context. There are some other things—curfew, what kind of clothes you wear, how you decorate your body, pierced ears, tattoos, those things—I won't go to the wall on those, because I don't have a level of authority that allows me to do it." Somewhere in the sermon, the speaker has the responsibility of making clear what authority is behind what he's saying.

**How often do you do that?**

With those people who hear me on a regular basis, I will share my pastoral wisdom from time to time. If I'm preaching one shot, I'm careful not to get off on the pastoral wisdom side too much, because I probably don't have the ethos to do that. But if it's people to whom I'm speaking frequently, every so often I let them know the rules (as explained above), or I will use some phrases so they will know, this is an absolute; that, on the other hand, is a little more tentative.

A lot of opinion passes for what people call topical preaching, and that has given topical preaching a bad name. Topical preaching can be and should be expository preaching. Topical preaching should be more than proof-texting, more than finding a word there that applies to some other word here, more than a situation taken out of context or irrelevant to our day. There's danger in that.

When you have the long lists of things related to a felt need—here are eight ways to get back on track after a divorce—and then pick a passage for each one of those, the messages usually are not expository topical preaching but good pastoral wisdom. You don't need a text to say that. My preference would be that we don't even pretend that this text teaches that—unless it clearly does.

**Let's not try to say that God is saying something when it's just me saying it.**

That's right. Let's not pretend God is saying it unless we can get into the text and demonstrate God is saying that.

**Timothy S. Warren** is professor of pastoral ministries at Dallas Theological Seminary and ministers to adults at Lake Pointe Church in Rockwall, Texas.

## 11

# MY FINGER ON THE HOT BUTTON

*Lessons from the abolitionist era on addressing controversial social issues.*

*John Henry Beukema*

Last year I took my wife to St. Louis on a holiday weekend. Mixing business with pleasure, we spent two and a half days in the Missouri Historical Research Library. My purpose was to research sermons from the mid-nineteenth century, specifically those addressing the topics of slavery and gambling.

I wanted to see how preachers dealt with the hot-button issues of the day, particularly in a border area like St. Louis. In the 1800s Missouri was a slave state, while Illinois was free. I intended to compare and contrast those sermons with how contemporary preachers approach social issues like abortion and gay marriage.

I came to the library planning to research from a list of six preachers from that place and time. The only name known to me was Edward Beecher, brother of Henry Ward Beecher and Harriet Beecher Stowe.

I searched books, personal letters, local newspapers, and other documents, many of them original manuscripts. The hunt failed to produce any sermons by those on my list of preachers, so I widened the search to all sermons from the mid-1800s. Amazingly I was unable to unearth a single printed sermon given in a church that focused on slavery or gambling.

Apparently such sermons once existed. For example, microfilm copies of the 1830s newspaper *The St. Louis Observer* referenced two antislavery sermons. The editor called them bold and well reasoned, but the degraded newsprint rendered the excerpts impossible for me to read.

One sermon by H. B. Bascom touched on both subjects, but only by way of application. In a collection of messages printed in 1849, *Sermons from the Pulpit* (a curiously redundant title for those days), Bascom declared, "The pulpit must not shrink from its duty." He then went on to blast a multitude of sins in a colorful way, including gambling and perhaps slavery, if that is what he meant by "the bigot, who hunts his fellow-being with the bitterness and ferocity of a fiend, and when his heartless unkindness has murdered him, would further assure himself he is right, but scenting the fancied smoke of his victim's torment ascending up forever and ever."

In the end I uncovered only one significant slavery sermon. It was not given in a church but at the Illinois State House, and it was a proslavery address. Rev. J. M. Peck delivered the message in Springfield on January 26, 1851. The Fugitive Slave Law was the hot-button issue of the moment. Although Illinois had become a free state about twenty-five years before, the state officials asked this pastor to prove to Christians that they should obey the government and return all fugitive slaves to their rightful owners. Peck responded with a stirring and scripturally based speech against abolitionists.

Several observations about sermons and the impact of preaching surfaced from my research.

## Most sermons are flashbulbs, not candles

Sermons themselves capture only a moment in time. Though they may reap eternal benefits in listeners' lives, most messages pass into earthly oblivion after the benediction. They provide a momentary flash for those present, and the bulb is discarded. Not that these sermons lack eternal significance; rather, God's purpose was served in that moment.

There was a reason the majority of sermons preached in nineteenth-century Missouri did not find their way into the museum. They were time stamped and culture sensitive. Those messages that did make it to print owed their preservation more to a preacher's worthy life than to the singular greatness of the sermons. Mary Greene, for example, was urged to pay tribute to her husband's ministry. She published a number of Jesse's sermons along with a short account of his life. David Coulter and William Humphrey Parks received similar honors. One hundred and fifty years later, the sermons themselves seemed unremarkable.

Sermons will have their greatest intended impact on one specific congregation. The best sermons are delivered by a faithful pastor to the people he knows and loves. Directed by the Spirit, the pastor expounds a specific text, at a specific time, that addresses a specific problem and meets a specific need. Even though that sermon could be preached in other churches, and the truths are true everywhere, most messages have the shelf life of a bag of manna.

Recently a couple told me how sorry they were to have to miss my sermon the next week. The woman said, "We'll get the CD, but it's never the same as being there." There is something to that. The Holy Spirit works and moves in that initial setting, communicating a message that doesn't always translate to tape, print, or MP3 files. I want every one of my sermons to burn brightly and eternally in the minds of those who hear, but longevity is not the litmus test of effectiveness. The Spirit may use this sermon as a brilliant flash that momentarily illumines and instructs and inspires, before fading away.

## Times change, but hermeneutical and homiletical mistakes remain constant

Most of the sermons I viewed for my research never left the biblical world. Using ornate and picturesque language, they described the experiences of the Israelites, the beauties of the temple, and justification by faith. The content was highly doctrinal, assuming a broad knowledge of the Bible and other classic literature. At times, the allusions, idioms, and quotations were effective, while some read like stilted, empty rhetoric. I found no reference to personal experiences, local events, national news, or current literature, and nothing that hinted at problems the hearers faced.

It reminded me of times my sermons surveyed the biblical territory and built a tower there, rather than a bridge to today's world. The opposite problem—never truly entering the biblical world while fully exegeting the modern one—is more common in our day, but no less mistaken.

Several of the preachers sounded much like the great Charles Haddon Spurgeon, who was shaking the world from his London pulpit during the last half of the nineteenth century. Of those, some seemed eerily similar in style, but without Spurgeon's passion or color or accessibility.

Yet who among us has not, consciously or unconsciously, emulated another preacher? Their speech patterns, style, or structure creep into our sermons. We do poor imitations of Ortberg or Warren or Piper, expressing truth through split personality.

In his proslavery sermon at the State House, Peck called for his abolitionist opponents to use a proper hermeneutic. "We must employ and interpret all language pertaining to laws, whether divine or human, according to the common use of words, and sound principles of interpretations." Referencing texts that abolitionists were using, Peck attempted to rescue those Scriptures from what he believed was a misapplication. His prime example was Acts 4:17–20, which he considered a "perversion" if applied to laws regulating the relationship of man to man. Peck said, "It was only when the government interfered with their religious rights—the duty they owed to God, that they were to resist, by patient endurance of persecution, even unto death."

I am personally familiar with this type of scriptural impropriety. Sadly, my record is not spotless when it comes to twisting the text to make a point, justify my position, or lessen my obligation to obey.

## True preaching is courageous enough to offend

I am passionate about taking the text seriously. I am passionate about personal authenticity and transparency. I am passionate about creativity and relevance. Preaching must be all that and more. Even so, one thing that can become diluted is courage. Not courage based on a misapplied text or instigated by a vocal majority, but courage to address difficult issues firmly, fully, and faithfully.

As I read Peck's sermon, I received a sudden stab of conviction. Praising a certain class of Baptists in the state, he talks of them being inoffensively antislavery. Among the plaudits he gives: "They never interfered, in an objectionable way, with the legal and political rights of slaveholders. They preached the gospel in an acceptable and successful manner, in slaveholding states." God help me, I never want to preach the gospel in an accepted and successful manner, by that definition. I wondered, "If I am not directly addressing the biggest problems of my time, can I truly be preaching the gospel?"

I don't believe it took much courage for Peck to preach his sermon. Invited by the government, he addressed a supportive audience, saying exactly what they asked him to say. Surely, even that Sunday, there were other pastors who spoke forcefully against the Fugitive Slave Law. Preachers did address this issue. Minds were changed about slavery, and Christians led the way, some suffering for their unpopular stand. Across the river from St. Louis, Rev. Elijah Lovejoy was murdered for his outspoken antislavery views. But none of those sermons are found in the Missouri Historical Research Library. Only a hermeneutically self-serving address, supporting the acceptable view, remains.

*Am I so wrapped up in correctly handling the text, being creative, relevant, clear, and likable that I fail to be dangerous?*

I wonder, "Do I have the courage to forgo historical preservation for courageous anonymity?" Most pastors want to be liked. I'm no different. Am I so wrapped up in correctly handling the text, being creative, relevant, clear, and likable that I fail to be dangerous? As a warning to myself I noted, "Avoid any and all temptation to preach for posterity, print, or praise."

My research was all too brief, uncovering little that related to my intended topic. Still, I found comfort in one thought. No temptation has seized me except what is common to preachers, even those of the nineteenth century.

I plan to return to St. Louis and revisit the research library. My wife will join me again, and I will treat her well. After all, someday she might want to publish some of my sermons.

**John Henry Beukema** is pastor of King Street Church in Chambersburg, Pennsylvania, and author of *Stories from God's Heart* (Moody). He served as associate editor of PreachingToday.com.

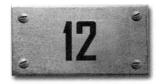

# 12

# THE LISTENER'S AGENDA

*When you are committed to the exposition of Scripture, what regard should you have for the felt needs of your hearers?*

*Bryan Chapell*

*One of the significant points of difference among preachers is the extent to which they are text driven, listener driven, or both. The caricature of the sequential expositors of Scripture is that they march through Scripture paragraph by paragraph preaching without regard for the listeners' real questions or the situations of their lives. Meanwhile the caricature of listener-driven preachers is that they think only of giving people what they want to hear out of a base desire simply to build a crowd. As noted expositor Bryan Chapell points out, we must have both the text and the listener keenly in view.*

**As any pastor knows, listeners have an agenda for our sermons. They have issues they'd like us to address. They have felt needs and questions they want us to talk about. How did Jesus and the apostle Paul treat the listener's agenda? And how is that relevant to what we should do?**

They recognized two things. One, listeners had an agenda that might or might not be in accord with God's agenda. Second, Jesus and Paul acted accordingly in that they certainly put God's agenda first, but they recognized God's agenda as seeking the hearts of men and women for Christ.

Therefore, while they had in mind the glory of God, they also had in mind the edification of his people. Keeping those two things together is the goal of good preaching. If preaching is directed only at God's glory, it becomes abstraction and arrogance. If it's only directed at people's edification, it becomes entertainment and in some ways just currying favor. What really serves God's people is when you are considering, how can I glorify God and edify his people at the same time?

**In the Bible, the ruler comes to Christ and asks, "What must I do to inherit eternal life?" Jesus responds. Is preaching similar to what Jesus does when he answers this man's specific question?**

Yes, although we don't always have Jesus' insight. In the ruler's case, our ready response would be, "Acknowledge that you are in need of a Savior and confess that Christ is Lord, and you will be saved." But Jesus sees a man who comes with all the accoutrements of riches and self-aggrandizement. The ruler's question indicates what's really in his heart: "What must *I* do to be saved?"

Jesus penetrates that by answering in a way that shocks us; he says, "Keep the commandments." It sounds like works-salvation to our ears, but you have to hear the question. The man had said, "What must *I* do to be saved?" Jesus penetrates the bubble the man has built by saying: if the question is what *you* do to be saved, then do everything.

The rich young ruler's response is, "All these commands I've kept from my youth." Jesus had just said that only God is good, and now three seconds later the young man says, me too. In doing so, he gives himself the status of God. What must Jesus do in that situation? He must make the man perceive his inability to be God. So he tells him impossible things to do, and finally the man turns away. What was Jesus doing? To let the man come on the basis of being good enough for God would actually be to damage him.

What Jesus does is speak to the necessities and the capacities of the individuals he is addressing. The necessity: the man must recognize his own insufficiency. His capacity: if Jesus just gives him a simple plan of salvation, he will not be able to understand what he is lacking. So Jesus must address the man at the level of his capacity to understand. Over and over again that is the balance of Scripture. It is not merely dealing with felt need. It's willing to do that at times, but in order that people who have low capacity may hear what is necessary for them to know.

> *Jesus speaks to the necessities and the capacities of the individuals he is addressing.*

Remember how Paul said to the Ephesian elders, "I have not hesitated to say anything needful to you for salvation." What does that "needful" mean? Paul says it's not just your felt needs. Sometimes I must address that. But I see beyond that to your godly needs, your biblical needs. And what ultimately is needed for your edification and for God's glory, that's what I will address. But that means I must deal with your capacity to hear me, as well as what you need to hear.

We are correct to hear our listeners even as we look at the Word. To say my job is simply to proclaim the Word, while turning a deaf ear to what my listeners are asking, is actually to damage them. What I'm doing is saying the Word does not really apply to their lives. I speak just into abstraction.

The best preachers are always doing two things at the same time. They are exegeting the text and exegeting their hearers. Not only do I consider what my hearers need to hear from this text, but I also consider what they are capable of hearing from this text. Have I put the fruit of the gospel within reach of those that God has given me to minister to? He has not only given me the Word to proclaim to these people, he has also given me these people to minister to. I must consider who they are, what they can hear, and what their needs are.

The old preacher's line says we need to remember we are preaching to sheep, not giraffes. If we preach to giraffes, we'll put things at a level we're comfortable with, or that our preaching peers are comfortable with, instead of listening to our hearers and saying, what are you capable of hearing?

If that sounds like compromise, remember that Jesus said to his own disciples: I have more to tell you, but you are not ready to receive it yet. He recognized that even though he had more truth to say, his disciples were not always at a level to receive it. So he had to speak at the level they could receive in order for them to grow in such a way that they could receive what they needed later.

Preachers debate about how to select their preaching texts. Should I preach consecutively through a book? Regardless of what people are experiencing, they're supposed to receive what they should from this text. On the other hand, should I identify what the people are struggling with and find a text that deals with that? My answer is both-and. It's not either-or.

Ralph Lewis described it years ago as the web and flow of preaching. Sometimes we flow. We move consecutively through a book or series of verses, knowing we will address issues that might not have come to our minds through our own experience. In this way, we preach the whole counsel of God.

At the same time, if there is the death of an elder in the church, an economic crisis in the community, or a natural disaster, for us to say, "I don't care about that. My obligation is to preach the next verse in this passage," is to say the Word of God doesn't really apply to life.

Instead, our preaching should at times have a web effect: when something significant has happened, I need to find the verse that captures it so I can deal directly with what my people are experiencing.

**We looked at an example from Jesus; let's focus now on Paul. In Corinthians Paul the apostle says, "Now, about the things you wrote about . . ." So he's dealing with questions that they have presented to him. They've said, "Paul, what do we do about this?" And here he writes a book of the Bible responding to the listeners' agenda. Again, how does that relate to our task as preachers?**

In 2 Timothy 4:2, Paul says, "Preach the Word; be prepared in season and out of season; correct, rebuke, and encourage." Those are all the straightforward, *Just preach it, man. Just do it.* But then he goes on to say, but do this "with great patience and careful instruction." There's the wonderful human touch. He says you have to do it with great patience. Be aware of the persons to whom you're talking. Some of them must take the truth out of eyedroppers, and some of them need to take it from fire hydrants. With great patience, discern whom you're talking to. And then, with great care, give them instruction.

He quickly follows that human touch by saying, but be careful because there will come a time when people will only want to gather around themselves teachers who "say what their itching ears want to hear."

Paul has done two things. He has said God sets the agenda: preach the Word. People don't set the agenda, since they are only able to determine what their own ears want to hear. But even as God sets the agenda, his agenda has in mind the care of his people. So pastoral care is considering what people need to hear, yes, but it's also considering the question, how can they hear it? How careful, how patient, how gentle, or, conversely, how strong and bold do you need to be for this truth to penetrate? It's the people's good as well as God's glory that set the agenda, not simply the people's desires.

**One definition of expository preaching is that it lets the Scripture text control the sermon. What should the preacher who is committed to that sort of exposition think about the listener's agenda? How much or in what ways should the listener's agenda control the preacher's agenda?**

I love that expository rubric, and I would not do anything but endorse it, because where the Bible speaks God speaks. So I'm attempting to simply reflect the truth of God as I preach in an expository way from the text. The text does have to control the truth that we speak. At the same time, as that truth's meaning is given, its significance will vary, given the people to whom I am speaking.

For example, if I'm speaking the truth from God's Word that God knows tomorrow, the significance of that truth may vary greatly for the hearers I'm addressing. If I'm addressing high schoolers concerned about where they will go to college next year—and whether God will still take care of them or if he knows tomorrow—I'm saying, even though you don't know where you will be next year, God knows. And that's why you can trust him.

But what if I'm speaking to folks in a nursing home, and they don't know if they will draw the next breath tomorrow or next year?

I'm speaking in two very different contexts, so that the significance of God's knowledge of tomorrow is different for the two crowds, but the truth is controlled by the text. So the meaning doesn't vary, but its significance may vary greatly according to the nature of my hearer.

**How does this affect the way we structure a sermon?**

We typically talk about the difference between the exegetical outline and the homiletical outline. Though there will be some differences in exegetical outlines, they shouldn't vary much from preacher to preacher. But the homiletical outline may vary greatly. Each preacher must ask: Which aspect of the text do I need to mention first to this particular congregation? What illustrations may I use? Of the minor or major points of the text, which needs the most emphasis for this group?

Maybe this group has never heard this before, or maybe this group has heard all of this before. My obligation is to exegete the text, but to be faithful to God's purpose I have to exegete the people as well and say: What do they need to hear? What can they hear? What do they most desire to hear? What do they not want to hear but must hear?

And if that sounds like compromising the text, we should remember what the father of expository preaching, John Broadus, said: the main thing to be done in preaching is application. He wasn't shortchanging exposition, but he was recognizing that the main goal of preaching is not information; it is transformation.

We have truth to say, but there is an end goal, and the end goal is changing the will and behavior of God's people for their edification.

**As I heard someone say once, our purpose is not just to get people into the Word; it's to get the Word into the people. So preachers can be so ideologically driven toward exposition that they can forget about their hearers and thereby do them a disservice. On the other hand, someone can be almost exclusively driven by the hearer. What do people on that end of the spectrum risk losing by being so listener driven?**

What you may lose if you are exclusively listener driven is, ultimately, the Word of God for God's people. The Word of God is meant to bring people the joy that is their strength. But at times people are taking their joy from the idols of the world. If we are not able to challenge, correct, even rebuke, then we will be driven by an agenda that is leading people into harm.

So the pastor has to have the objective distance of the Scriptures setting the agenda. I have to say what the Scripture says because it, more than I, knows what is good for God's people. By being faithful to the truth of the text, I challenge the idols of the times and the idols in people's hearts and say at times what their itching ears do not want to hear. If I only follow their agenda, I may be led to issues too shallow. I may be led to issues actually secular and wrong. I may be led to say things in such a way that people, while they are pleased with what I am saying, are not displeased enough with their sin to turn from it.

There are certain rights that people have in the pew. One is that the pastor will address what is going on in their lives. But I must do so in a way that is true to the Scriptures more than simply true to their desires.

**Bryan Chapell** is president of Covenant Theological Seminary in St. Louis, Missouri, where he also serves as professor of practical theology. He is author of *Christ-Centered Preaching* (Baker).

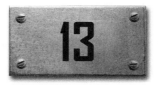

# 13

# RIVETING SERMONS

*How to get and keep the listeners' attention.*

*Jeffrey Arthurs*

Of the thousands of sermons I've heard in my lifetime, I remember only a few; but those few glitter in my memory like diamonds scattered on a beach. One of the brightest did not shine with humor (though I recall laughing at points), nor did it shine with a showy delivery (though I distinctly remember the passion in the preacher's voice). That sermon riveted my attention because the preacher spoke about something vital to me. He exhorted us to "guard our hearts, for the heart is the wellspring of life," and you could hear a feather drop in the sanctuary, because my church had just lost our worship leader, who was having an affair. We sensed we could fall just as the worship leader had.

Every sermon cannot, indeed should not, strive to be a once-in-a-lifetime sermon. But every sermon should rivet attention on the Word. How can we increase the level of attention granted our sermons? Here is a clue.

On Thanksgiving Day, my family and I visited Old Sturbridge Village in central Massachusetts. This town re-creates

New England life in the year 1837. Actors in authentic costumes role-play to give tourists a feel for that era. Only a few tourists dialogued with the banker, lawyer, or minister. Instead, the crowds gathered in a dining room at noon to watch our New England ancestors eat Thanksgiving dinner. Dozens of tourists packed themselves into a stuffy room for a vicarious feast of turkey, potatoes, squash, pies, and cider. The smells and sights riveted our attention. My stomach growled as I watched the actors—who were obviously enjoying this part of their jobs.

Why did the crowds gather to watch the meal while only three or four people dialogued with the Congregationalist minister? Because we were hungry. When people are hungry, they pay attention to food. So it is with a sermon. In *Desiring God*, John Piper argues that humans are hungry. We crave joy. Deep needs for security and significance reside in every heart. When preachers surface needs such as these and demonstrate how God meets them, they rivet attention.

Here are three ways to identify deep needs. These are more than techniques; they must be a lifestyle.

## Listen to your neighbors

Listen to your neighbors' prayer requests—broken health, wayward children, jobless breadwinners. Preach to the suffering, and you will never lack an audience. Listen to your neighbors talk about money, relationships, recreation, death, and truth. Listen to the subtext: their attitudes. Can money give security? In your sermon, illustrate this and offer real security.

I understand that Bill Hybels often does sermon prep in the coffee shop or locker room. He sits and thinks, "How would these people respond to my central idea? What objections would they raise? What misconceptions do they have?" I have a friend who opens his pictorial church directory and "listens" to so-and-so air her opinions on his thesis.

## Listen to yourself

What do you care about? You care about the same things all humans care about: security and significance. While it is true that preachers find these commodities in places our listeners rarely venture (like the Septuagint and PreachingToday.com), all of us are trying to satisfy the same hunger. Apply the Word to yourself, and it will likely apply to your people in the same way.

For example, one thought that has crossed my mind more than once is, will I have the same standard of living when I retire as I do now? I am confident God will meet my needs when I'm old and gray, but, frankly, I hope he also meets my wants! When I include that concern in a sermon, I'm confident others will identify with me.

*Apply the Word to yourself, and it will likely apply to your people in the same way.*

## Listen to authors

When you read, pay attention to the subtext of attitudes, values, and beliefs. Magazines sell because they address issues we care about. Fiction sells because it deals with universal themes.

I'm currently listening to a recording of *A Connecticut Yankee in King Arthur's Court* by Mark Twain, and I'm learning much about the American ethos. *Democracy, equality,* and *achievement* are foundational terms for us. Someday I know I'll talk about that in a sermon.

Whether listening to a sermon or touring a nineteenth-century village, hungry people pay attention to food. To gain attention and feed the flock, preachers must speak to the vital needs of their listeners.

**Jeffrey Arthurs** is the professor of preaching and communication, and the chair of the division of practical theology, at Gordon-Conwell Theological Seminary.

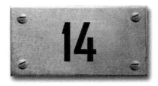

# 14

# TOO HOW-TO

*When an engaging sermon form turns wooden.*

*John Henry Beukema*

Perhaps you've heard the story of the young man who went to the library and spotted a book titled *HOW to HUG*. Interested in this provocative heading, he took it home. It wasn't until he tried to read the book that the man discovered it was merely volume 7 of the encyclopedia.

Just as *HOW to HUG* is an incomplete portion of the encyclopedia, the how-to sermon is only one of many ways to preach. Although how-to sermons can be biblical and appealing, a steady diet may become tedious or, worse, distort the text.

What qualifies as a how-to sermon?

## Four characteristics of how-to sermons

### 1. The how-to sermon is prescriptive

Prescriptions are necessary. Every day I take a medication prescribed by my neurologist. The medicine prevents seizures, and without it I wouldn't be able to drive or swim. My doctor diagnosed a problem and prescribed a solution. How-to preaching does the same. It says, "Here is what's wrong, and here's how to fix it." Obviously this is a necessary part of preaching. We point out the human condition, sin and separation from God, and then offer God's solution, salvation, and reconciliation through Christ.

Some examples of prescriptive sermon titles would be "Getting Right with God," "How to Find Peace," "Five Steps to Improve Your Marriage," and "Secrets to Financial Security."

**2. The how-to sermon is practical**

While messages on supralapsarianism do not readily fit into the practical category, a how-to sermon deals with everyday issues. It focuses on subjects most people recognize as necessary to their lives. Practicality is a good thing. Many passages of Scripture offer useful counsel on ordinary matters, common to human experience. Examples of practical sermon titles would be "Five Steps to Forgiving Others" and "How to Be a Godly Parent."

**3. The how-to sermon is relevant**

Who among us doesn't want to hear, "Pastor, you spoke directly to me; that was just what I needed today"? God's Word is supremely relevant. All of Scripture, even the genealogies and lists of temple items, is ultimately applicable to us. How-to sermons make a felt need the main focus. Because of that, such a sermon can feel intensely relevant and significant to the hearer. Examples of relevant sermon titles would include "How to Deal with Discouragement" and "Overcoming Your Fears."

**4. The how-to sermon is didactic**

Moral instruction is evident in such a message. It may be presented in the form of, if you do *X,* then *Y* will happen. For example, take the title "How to Be Holy." A didactic sermon would give three attitudes or four ways or seven steps to achieving greater holiness. In "Choosing Relationship over Religion," the how-to sermon might identify the traits of religion as opposed to genuine faith. It may be presented: if you find yourself at *A*, and you need to get to *Z*, here's how.

None of these characteristics necessarily signal danger. However, the how-to sermon form does have a potential downside. Here are four possible concerns.

## Downsides of how-to sermons

### 5. How-to sermons may ignore genre

The bulk of Scripture is actually in narrative form. While some of that may be used prescriptively, not all of it can be. To do so would be similar to taking a feature-length movie and turning it into an instructional video. Lord of the Rings becomes a series on Guidelines for Withstanding Evil. Genesis was not handed down to us as a list of propositions. Jesus could have said, "Here are three attitudes you need to have to truly love your neighbor." Instead, he told a story. Narratives can be principlized, but to do so in every case may obscure the plot.

Approaching everything in a how-to fashion will not give biblical poetry the honor it is due. Developing the beautiful imagery of Psalm 23 into "Ways to Experience God as Shepherd" may not be the best technique for handling the text. We do not communicate poetry to full effect through a list of principles or instructions.

### 6. How-to sermons may subvert the point of the text

The point of the text may be more about *who* or *why* than *how*. We can draw how-to points from a text that may have validity or at least be consistent with biblical principles stated elsewhere, but we may be answering a question not intended in the text.

For example, using God the Father's words of approval at the baptism of Jesus as a guideline for good parenting is obviously not the main thrust of the text.

Since we believe the Bible is God's Word, we view all of it as profitable for us. It is because we take the text seriously that we can mistakenly grab for a how-to approach that may contradict the text's purpose.

Consider the somewhat introductory material of Romans 1:8–15. One expositor with a high view of Scripture selected that portion of the chapter and developed principles of good leadership. To whatever extent that is a legitimate secondary application, it may detract from the thrust of Paul's passion for the power of the gospel, culminating in verses 16 and 17.

### 7. How-to sermons may ignore emotion

The practicality and didactic elements of such sermons tend to focus more on the head than the heart. How-to sermons can fall victim to a lack of passion or fail to evoke an emotional response in the hearer. It is the difference between saying, "I love you," and, "Take two aspirin and call me in the morning." Both can be said with deep concern and feeling. The difference is that one expresses an emotion, the other an instruction. One is relational, the other directional. When it comes to the biblical text, how-to sermons focus more on the latter than the former.

Take Genesis 1, for example. When reading that text in our day, one of the more prominent concerns might be the issue of creation versus evolution. But to address themes like "Seven Reasons to Be a Creationist" or "How God Created the Universe" would be to miss what the text shows about the joy and wonder of creation. Preaching the creation account should not leave people primarily thinking, "God really did do it." Instead, there should be a sense of awe and wonder in our majestic, powerful God who made all things good. The Bible contains some passages that are meant to be emotionally evocative more than they are to be instructive. How-to sermons may neglect that emphasis.

**8. How-to sermons may become human centered**

Every text is not about me and my needs. Ultimately every text is about God. To focus constantly on the *how* can subtly influence our perspective of Scripture. For example, the awe-inspiring scene from Isaiah 6:1–4 should probably not be a sermon titled "How to Meet with God." There is nothing doctrinally wrong with that; it simply turns a God-centered passage into a human-centered one.

> *Every text is not about me and my needs.*

Dave is a friend of mine who admits to disliking reading. He finds it a challenge to go through a Bible study book and would never read a novel. However, he does enjoy reading technical manuals. Whereas I won't even bother to read the instructions before putting something together, he loves to discover how things operate and devours mechanical and engineering books in his spare time. Dave recently sent me a book titled *How Candles Work*. He wanted to share his joy of discovery with me. I found about two and a half chapters interesting. The remaining seven chapters were simply a jumble of equations and scientific principles that brought candle lighting to the level of anesthesia.

There is a line between useful, interesting information and tedious dissection of the laws of thermodynamics. How-to preaching has its place. But there are times when, instead of explaining how it works, the sermon should simply light the candle.

**John Henry Beukema** is pastor of King Street Church in Chambersburg, Pennsylvania, and author of *Stories from God's Heart* (Moody). He served as associate editor of PreachingToday.com.

# A HEART FOR SERMON APPLICATION

*Seven guidelines for tuning application to yourself and your specific hearers.*

*Joshua Harris*

Much of my preaching style has been influenced by my mentor C. J. Mahaney, the head of the Sovereign Grace ministry. He took me under his wing when I was still traveling for one-day events as a conference speaker. His example is what inspired me to invest my life in the local church. I want to affect the way people apply truth to their lives. When you live in a community, you see the effect of that application.

Here are seven principles that guide my sermon application.

**1. My thoughts are often directed toward different groups of people**

I've learned to ask questions about my audience from Mark Dever, pastor of Capitol Hill Baptist Church in Washington. He has a chart that walks through different categories of people. "What will the unsaved person take away? What about the strong Christian? What about the new Christian?" I don't honestly go through a checklist myself when I'm preparing a message, but I do keep real people in mind. I ask, "What does this mean for *them*?"

There are certain messages that lend themselves to that more easily than others. First Corinthians, for example—there's rich potential for application in that book. But it's not always quite as clear and simple as a message on materialism, which I know each and every person deals with in some way.

### 2. Sermon application must come from a pure heart

I have to fight sinful desires in my own heart to impress people or other pastors. I have to come back to a root desire to be faithful to the Word. I have to ask what difference my words will make for people who are going to work on Monday morning.

John Stott's book *Between Two Worlds* encourages me. He emphasizes preparing a sermon on your knees, praying over your words and over your people. I want to grow in this. It brings the preparation process back not to my skillful structure, but to God's breath of life. That is the most important thing that we can do as preachers.

### 3. Application happens throughout the sermon

There was a time when application in my preaching was loaded at the end: "truth" came at the beginning of the sermon, "application" at the end. Sometimes I still preach that way because of the text's structure, but I now realize that application should happen throughout the message. It doesn't need to be separate from exposition.

I ask what best serves people based on the way the passage unfolds.

**4. Application does not always mean to do something**

Certain passages are easier to apply, and I don't feel that I need the same richness of application in every single message. Sometimes I need to trust God's Word and understand that people don't always need a specific, direct application point to benefit from Scripture.

I'm a big believer in the importance of application, but I also recognize that there are going to be messages where it's not "go and do this." Some messages are more "here's truth; let's revel in it, and let it adjust our thinking." Different passages prompt different responses.

**5. Application begins with my own personal obedience**

Paul exhorted Timothy, "Watch your life and doctrine closely." The starting point for us as preachers is to live our sermons first. Unless we apply God's Word in our own lives, that well is going to run dry. It's vital for me—like the rest of my church—to be in a small group, to pursue fellowship with other men, to talk about sin in my life, and to receive biblical truth from my community. If I don't apply what I know is true, I'm not going to be conformed to the image of Christ.

I think so many pastors use illustrations of their children because in them we see the working out of the truth on a simple level. There are many times when I realize that the things I say to my kids are really just biblical application. I need to exhort my congregation to respond as children to a good heavenly Father.

I network with other preachers, and sometimes my preaching network will send around an e-mail saying, "I'm preaching on this topic. Can you help me think of examples?"

Sometimes you can sense the danger of a message becoming formulaic and stale. In those cases, it's helpful to push on through. You might be preaching to a teen who has never grappled with the topic. Perhaps there's a stay-at-home mom listening who is now in a season of life when the message applies. It's helpful to walk through those scenarios in your mind and think about how this truth would be applied to them.

First Timothy 4:16, "Watch your life and doctrine closely. . . . because if you do, you save both yourself and your hearers," is a powerful reminder that we need to get the doctrine right, but if we're not living this, we will be leading people astray. Ultimately our practice is going to work back into our teaching.

**6. I must continually work at knowing what the real issues and questions are for my people**

In a relatively large church like ours we can become disconnected from the real-life situations and circumstances of our members. We interact primarily with other Christians, many of them church leaders.

> *It's an ongoing challenge for me to interact with where people really are and not just where I think they are.*

It's an ongoing challenge for me to interact with where people really are and not just where I think they are. We need to interact with people who are not believers. But this same principle can apply to our members. We create an image of who we're talking to. We might just be talking to ourselves in our sermons. When we do this, we forget what they're really asking, what they're really struggling with, the lies they believe, and the temptations they face.

We love to have folks over at our home. We'll just invite a random sampling of people, get them together, and enjoy talking about what's going on in their hearts, in our small groups, in the church at large. As I hear them state things in their own words, I find myself thinking, "Oh, that's what's really happening. Oh, that's what people are really thinking."

This is very helpful when I'm phrasing application. Sometimes it's not only telling people what the application is, but it's removing barriers. It's saying, "God's telling us to do this. Now I know you're probably thinking such and such, because I know the temptation is to think this."

Acknowledging the challenges to thought and practice in this way is powerful. I've had people say, "Thank you for saying that, because I was thinking that. Your honesty helped me to hear the truth and softened my heart."

**7. I try to give people specific action steps**

C. J. Mahaney has taught the passage in James about the person who looks in the mirror and walks away unchanged. His hilarious description of this passage is burned in my mind. He says how unfortunate it would be if people looked in the mirror on Sunday morning and didn't make any adjustments before they came to church. What if they didn't comb their hair and didn't take the guck out of their eyes? He brought that mirror analogy home to us.

That is a defining principle in my thinking about application. I'm holding up a mirror for people to look into. It's not enough for me to point out to them what the mirror shows. I also need to give them a plan. I need to put the comb in their hand. I need to give them a washbasin. They need not only a description, but also a pathway to change as they respond to the truth they see. That is what I want to do in every sermon I preach.

**Joshua Harris** is senior pastor of Covenant Life Church in Gaithersburg, Maryland, and the author of *Stop Dating the Church* (Multnomah).

16

# SERMON APPLICATION IN A POST-CHRISTIAN CULTURE

*Bringing the Bible to bear on the lives of people who think authority is a bad word.*

*Lyle Dorsett, John Koessler, James MacDonald, Steve Nicholson, and John Henry Beukema*

*We preach in a culture where biblical authority is not assumed, but questioned. In this environment, the task of applying God's truth can be increasingly difficult. To help with this challenge, PreachingToday.com gathered a group of experienced preachers into a recording studio in Carol Stream, Illinois, to discuss their approach to application in a post-Christian society.*

**We live in a culture in which a greater percentage of believers and seekers have grown up without moral training, without agreed-upon moral bearings, and without a belief in the moral authority of Scripture. How does this affect sermon application? What challenges arise as we try to bridge from the principles of Scripture to people living in a culture in moral chaos?**

**John Koessler:** We're preaching to a culture that believes morality and truth are experientially determined. They gain their own sense of what's right and wrong on a subjective level. As a preacher, I'm coming from the perspective that truth is objective. I'm preaching from a base of authority, and that creates a conflict for me.

For example, if I argue from Scripture without appealing to experience, it lacks validity for the listener. If I preach solely from experience, it lacks authority. As a preacher, I have to keep my feet in both areas. I must stand on the base of biblical authority and propositional truth, but I also have to keep a foot in the listeners' experience so they recognize the validity of what I have to say.

**Steve Nicholson:** If you give people the right kind of application to show how Scripture has power to change their lives, they can come to recognize that authority, even though they haven't started there.

**Koessler:** What do you start with: experience or authority?

**Nicholson:** I start with the Scripture, helping hearers see it's telling us about people who experienced God working in their lives. It's starting with experience, but it's the experience of those in Scripture. That makes it real for people.

**Lyle Dorsett:** It's imperative that we speak from Scripture. Sometimes I'll say, "You might not agree with this now, but file this away, because when the way you're living ceases to work, you will have a genuine alternative."

I use experiential examples. For example, I'll say, "Sin is fun for a season. I can still remember when the chandeliers glistened and the glasses tinkled, and people were laughing and having a good time. Then I remember waking up with vomit on my shoes and wondering where I was."

Scripture offers me a genuine alternative. The church that makes me feel comfortable by imitating the world doesn't actually make me comfortable at all when the Spirit has convicted me that I am wretched and I need help.

**James MacDonald:** Does the Bible have to be recognized as an authority in the mind of the hearer in order for the Scripture to make an impact? I would answer emphatically no. Scripture is a supernatural book. We make much of the messenger. The messenger is little; the message is much. The Spirit of God taking the message can penetrate the heart of the most persistent of pagans.

**Koessler:** The foundation of preaching must be the authority of biblical truth. But at the same time, I don't believe it's magic, where all I need to do is stand on the street corner, read the Bible, and people will be magically converted when they hear the words. I mediate truth as a preacher. I don't just throw it as a projectile.

**MacDonald:** I don't believe the Bible is magical, but I believe the Bible is powerful in its proclamation. We've lost a proclamation theology in the church. It's not reading it on the corner but proclaiming it on the corner that God will bless. I call for the sovereignty of the message, not the sovereignty of the audience.

The preacher has to be gripped with the message. When someone preaches and is gripped by the urgency, necessity, and eternity of the message, the cultural readiness of Person X becomes fairly insignificant.

**Nicholson:** I've been preaching in a postmodern setting for twenty-eight years. The vast majority in my audience don't accept the authority of Scripture. Yet we always start with the Scripture. We let them see its power. Again and again we've seen them come to accept its authority.

**Koessler:** What do you mean by "start with the Scripture"? The foundation for my message is what the text has to say, but I tell my homiletics students to start with the experience of the audience in the introduction and use that as a bridge to the Scripture.

When you consider Paul's preaching on Mar's Hill, he clearly has a sense of his audience and adjusts the approach of his message. He preaches to Jews one way; he preaches to Gentiles another way. Not a different message but a different focus. On Mar's Hill he's preaching to Greek philosophers and doesn't reference Scripture.

Having said that, though, one of the grievances I have with some of the sermons coming from the seeker context is how much distance from Scripture there is in those messages. The end result is a lot of application and even truth principles but no biblical foundation. It's a motivational speech, not a sermon.

**Dorsett:** Ultimately when you preach, you're going to point to Jesus. You can't avoid it. When Paul says, "Let me tell you about this other God you're looking for," he's pointing to Jesus. The most seeker-friendly thing we can do for sick souls is get them into the presence of Jesus Christ, and it's going to require Scripture to do that.

*The most seeker-friendly thing we can do for sick souls is get them into the presence of Jesus Christ, and it's going to require Scripture to do that.*

**MacDonald:** We are far too conscientious about our interpretation preparation and not as equally conscientious about our application preparation. I spend 50 percent of my time in message preparation on application. I think, "How am I going to say this to people? How can they see it in their lives?"

With regard to the importance of sound proclamation theology, though, what I'm sounding the alarm against is the tendency to remove our sermons from the place where the power is in the interest of reaching nonbelievers.

**One reason we face a sense of greater moral chaos today is that we address moral questions, such as entertainment choices, that Scripture does not speak about directly. How do we speak to issues not specifically addressed in Scripture?**

**John Beukema:** I'm not an issues preacher; I start with a text, not with a subject. The issues Scripture doesn't directly address are all possible applications. A common mistake preachers can make is to bring out applications that don't have an honest connection to the text. That undermines biblical authority, both for the believer and for the person who doesn't even believe it has authority. If I'm preaching from Romans 13 where it says the commandments are don't steal, don't covet, love does no harm to its neighbor, I think addressing copyright laws and illegal file sharing are pertinent applications.

As a preacher, I'm always in the hunt for an application of my text; I'm not hunting for texts for my applications.

**Koessler:** One of the struggles in preaching is a tendency for a preacher to lose sight of the text when you move to application. It takes discipline to keep the text in view while thinking through what the implication is for the audience.

**Beukema:** Since Sunday is always coming and my big concern is "what is this going to mean? how does this intersect with our lives?" I mustn't jump there too quickly. I struggle to be patient. I do the work and wait on the Spirit. Rushing to application too early brings inauthentic applications.

**Koessler:** Sometimes we forget that the original audience of the text faced the same fundamental questions in life that we're wrestling with. Why do we die? Why can't we get along with each other? With all that I have, why am I still not satisfied? The specific application the biblical author addresses might be removed from our cultural context, but the fundamental life questions are the same. If I can connect with those principles, it's easier for me to link some unstated specifics to my text in application.

**A high percentage of people today try cohabitation before marriage. Scripture doesn't say you can't smoke marijuana. How do you deal with issues like these?**

**Nicholson:** Let people see that Scripture speaks to those things when it talks about being pure or about being sober. Then they have to understand why God says it. God protects the importance of marriage, because without marriage you end up with a lot of women and children being abused and in poverty.

I start by letting them see what the Bible says, and then I want them to see that God is saying this for good reason. It's for freedom, for protection, not to kill your joy. It's a positive thing. The culture tells people they don't have a choice. I want to tell them that's not true. You do have a choice. I give them hope that they can have a better way of living.

**Dorsett:** I begin with the presupposition that I'm called to do more than teach. Teaching isn't the primary task of the sermon. The primary task is to get people into the presence of Christ and let him change them.

I must address issues my congregation is dealing with, such as masturbation and pornography. It has to be addressed by preaching about faithfulness to your wife or faithfulness to God.

You call people to consider what idols have to be torn down, so that Christ can take his rightful place. We have to directly confront these things because people know what they're doing is not working. They know they're in prison.

**Do you frame your answer in terms of "this is my view," or do you say, "the Bible says"?**

**Dorsett:** I say I believe this is a biblical position, and I believe two thousand years of tradition will support how we understand this.

**MacDonald:** The question implies the preacher has a responsibility to answer every question life raises. Peter said that in God's Word we have all things pertaining to life and godliness.

My experience is that the Holy Spirit is faithful in producing a point of conviction on everything that's sin. Everything God forbids, he forbids for your greater joy. I can't even preach all the stuff the Bible does talk about, so I don't see myself spending much time on what it doesn't address. I tell our pastors, don't spend your authority on everything. Spend your authority on "thus saith the Lord." Otherwise you weaken your authority, and people think you're just fired up about everything.

In seeking to answer questions, the whole truth gives information to answer the questions. Application is then the body of truth and how it is directed to various points of morality or whatever. Messages *about* the subject are very different from points of application into that sphere.

**Koessler:** The kinds of issues not explicitly mentioned in Scripture are things that end up in the periphery of the sermon.

Foundational truth at its heart gives us the truth principles that fuel all application. Then as we're applying that to the audience, we're going to think situationally. These issues don't become the center of the message, but we move out from the center to help the audience address these various questions that Scripture doesn't explicitly address.

**What is the place of pastoral wisdom in sermon application? By pastoral wisdom I mean sermon applications not specifically taught in Scripture that are based on wisdom gleaned from experience, observation, discernment, social science, research data, and the like. For example, if you had a problem in the past with pornography, I suggest you never go to a secular bookstore by yourself. That would be what I would call pastoral wisdom application.**

**Nicholson:** I like the approach of seeing different levels of application. Give people enough specifics so they think, "I could do that."

I will often use "for instances": "this is what this truth could mean in school; this is what that could mean at work." The difficulty with being too specific is then you have a small percentage of your congregation that relates to it and a big percentage that doesn't. I will try to hit enough different contexts so most people can draw out implications.

**MacDonald:** I use what I call transitional content, lists of insights gathered and gleaned over twenty years of pastoral ministry.

For example, recently I preached a series on David's life. In the first message, I dealt with the call of David. Here's a guy who was out taking care of the sheep, a little boy. Who would have thought such an ordinary person doing an ordinary job would ever be king? The transitional content before we got to application was "five identity lies the world speaks and the church parrots." They were lies like you are unique; you are your job; you are your past, and so on. I didn't get this list from the Bible. I got that from life observation. It was undergirded by a foundation of biblical truth. I backed up every one of the points from Scripture. I use that transitional content to give people places to hang up the application.

**So you're saying, here's what the Scripture says; here's how that interacts with the things going on in our world—what's believed, what's said, what's done. And that takes pastoral wisdom to make the connection.**

**MacDonald:** Yes, it is insight into the text and then insight into life. In the gift of preaching, there is a capacity to make that connection for people, to take this truth and plug it into life. Seeing those connections and then communicating them are two different components of preaching giftedness.

**Philippians 4:8 and 2 Corinthians 7:1 are examples of passages that open the door wide for application. Second Corinthians 7:1 calls us to cleanse ourselves from every defilement of body and spirit. What does defile body and spirit? It doesn't tell us here. What sort of application would you make on such passages? What would be out of bounds?**

**Koessler:** Neither of those passages is entirely open-ended. In 2 Corinthians 1, for example, Paul's talking about how the promise that God will one day claim us as his own should affect our allegiance in the here and now. In the Corinthian context, it has to do with the questions of belonging. Whom do I identify with? Whom should I listen to?

I first try to understand the context in which that statement is made and then ask myself, what are the corollary questions for my audience? I'm going to flesh that out in specific situational examples. Then I take the principle and suggest that for some people it's going to look like this; for other people it's going to look like this—and then go back to the principle.

**What would be out of bounds as an application from 2 Corinthians 7:1?**

**Koessler:** That passage has been used inappropriately as a catchall for any behavior I don't like. Extreme forms of separationism use that verse in a way not entirely consistent with what Paul is talking about.

**How do we make the decisions about what would qualify for that principle and what wouldn't?**

**Koessler:** You start with the text. When I start to identify my categories of situations that I think relate to that, do they fit into that particular scriptural context? If they don't, I have to become tentative about the degree of force I give to that.

**Nicholson:** Second Corinthians 7:1 is about a mentality you have to bring people to. The danger is that if you make too big of a jump to specific application, you shoot the shotgun that goes everywhere but nowhere. What they need is the mentality described here, not just the application, "I shouldn't do this or that."

**MacDonald:** When I am under time pressure and I haven't given it the time I need, I tend to do the shotgun thing. Shotgun is easy. It's fast, and it does hit people. If it doesn't kill anyone, it definitely wounds a lot of people. It's better to choose two or three core things from 2 Corinthians 7. Here are some arenas that reflect a life of separation. Here are the consequences we pay for a lack of separation, and here are the benefits that we forgo through a lack of separation. Here are some ways we could be stronger in this category and help one another. Drilling deeper on a couple of things is a lot harder work.

**Koessler:** In Philippians 4:8, Paul seems satisfied to leave it as a general principle. As important as I feel concrete application is, sometimes we put too much of a burden on ourselves and end up giving people a grocery list. More often than not in Scripture, you're given a general principle, and what we need to do is not spelled out with precision. Paul, who was himself a preacher, at times makes pointed, specific application, and at other times simply states a general principle. My role as a preacher is to stand between the text and the audience to mediate the text. I have an obligation to do the hard work of raising implications. But sometimes the best application is simply the general principle.

**Dorsett:** Paul gives us an illustration here. He tells us what to do. Start focusing on what is true, honorable, just, rather than on things that defile you.

I use an illustration that D. L. Moody frequently used. I pick up a tumbler full of muddy water and say, "This is my soul. Look at the filth in it. It's ugly. If you get up every day and look at that and think, 'This looks terrible. God, forgive me. This is awful,' all you're going to do is get obsessed with it, and nothing's going to change."

Then I pick up a pitcher of clear water and pour the clear water into the muddy-water-filled tumbler and begin to displace it.

Here we have 2 Corinthians telling us what to avoid. We have Paul in Philippians 4 telling us what to do. I tell my guys, "You want to get pornography out of your heart? You want to get this filth out? Start singing praises. Turn on a different kind of music. You've got to purposely fill your mind with stuff to displace the garbage."

**Ministries like Teen Challenge that treat people who have had life-controlling addictions and lived in moral chaos seem to have to make strict rules for people. In sermon application in a post-Christian culture, what place is there for making for believers rules not found in Scripture, such as never attend an R-rated movie, never attend an X-rated movie, or whatever level you want to put on that? If there is a need for rules because of the moral chaos of our culture, how do we avoid legalism, Pharisaism?**

**Nicholson:** The danger is that you get compliance to rules but no real heart change, and then you have legalism. I want people to make the right choices without having to refer back to a rule. They become spiritually sensitized so that if they see something bad for them, they decide, "I'm not going to do that," as opposed to, "The pastor said don't go to thus and so movie." It's the difference between change and compliance. People can get fixated on a specific and miss the main thing. If you start giving a lot of rules, they will get fixated on the rules and generally take them further than you actually set. If you say, "This is a rule," it generates rule keeping, and people start going through a checklist without a clear connection to the state of the heart.

**Koessler:** When we're talking about things not clearly stated in Scripture, it's a question of whether you state it with the force of law. The clearer the connection to the principle, the stronger the force can be. You can give the rule. The further away you are from the principle, the more tentative you must be. You may have to state it as a preference: this is my rule. Or as a suggestion: you may want to adopt this rule. But you can't state it with the force of law.

**MacDonald:** Legalism is an extrabiblical code of conduct and the judging of others' spirituality on whether they adhere to the code. It isn't wrong to have rules. It isn't wrong for Teen

Challenge to have a community of faith that agrees to a code of conduct. Legalism would be for someone from Teen Challenge to meet someone who isn't part of the Teen Challenge community and judge their spirituality based on whether or not they conform to the extrabiblical code.

I preach with conviction the things I feel certain about from Scripture. I don't equivocate on those, because Jesus never equivocated. There are some major issues about which Christians cannot agree to disagree, and then there are a large number of other issues about which Christians need to show respect for the larger body of Christ.

**Koessler:** That's the difference between fundamentals and distinctives. But I don't want to imply that distinctions are unimportant. In evangelicalism we give the impression that, pretrib, midtrib, posttrib, it's all pretty much the same. It's not all the same. One of those views is right, or none of those views is right, but there is a certain point when Jesus is going to come back. We acknowledge the distinctives and treat one another with respect, but we also have to say that we shouldn't hold to a theological relativism that just accepts them all. Somebody's right and somebody's wrong.

**MacDonald:** There's confusion about who are our partners. Anybody today who believes in the substitutionary atonement of Christ as the only basis for the new birth and in the authority of God's Word is our partner in building God's kingdom.

I can have a great debate with Lyle about modes of baptism, but what would edify me is that we would be having a discussion about, what does the Bible actually teach? There are large numbers of people in the body of Christ today who find the discussion about what the Bible actually teaches as an irrelevancy, something that doesn't really matter. That is the front on which we need to be joining arms and defending ourselves against the advance of that position, because there is no future for preaching if that onslaught carries the day. Preach the Word, and all application needs to flow from that.

**John Henry Beukema** is pastor of King Street Church in Chambersburg, Pennsylvania, and author of *Stories from God's Heart* (Moody). He served as associate editor of PreachingToday .com. **Lyle Dorsett** is Billy Graham Professor of Evangelism at Beeson Divinity School in Birmingham, Alabama, and author of *Seeking the Secret Place* (Brazos). **John Koessler** is professor and chair of the Pastoral Studies Department at Moody Bible Institute in Chicago and author of *Folly, Grace, and Power* (Zondervan). **James MacDonald** is pastor of Harvest Bible Chapel in Rolling Meadows, Illinois, and host of *Walk in the Word*, a daily thirty-minute radio program heard on outlets across North America. He is author of *Always True* (Moody). **Steve Nicholson** is pastor of Vineyard Christian Fellowship of Evanston, in Evanston, Illinois, and national coordinator of church planting for Vineyard USA.

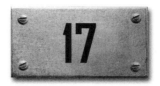

# 17

# PRESSURED TO PROMOTE

*Are church leaders twisting your arm to support their ministries from the pulpit? Here's how to lead the church and remain faithful to the Scriptures.*

*Timothy J. Peck*

Many leaders in the church where I minister believe that unless I as the preacher promote their ministry it will fail. In just one recent week, various church leaders asked me to promote from the pulpit our student ministry, missions budget, small group ministry, and children's ministry. They count on me to be their public advocate. How are preaching pastors to respond to these expectations?

We could simply ignore these requests. For my first five years of preaching, that was my tack. "I'm called to preach the Bible," I responded, "so your ministry is going to have to succeed without my public promotion." My response was inadequate, because it failed to understand that preaching is an act of leadership. To fail to address the church's ministries in preaching implies that the preacher has no leadership stake in these ministries. This response encourages ministries to become special-interest groups, producing competition for resources.

Another response is to promote ministries when you feel pressured to do so. Your children's ministry director paints a dire picture of what will happen if more volunteers are not recruited, so before your sermon you take a few minutes to ask for volunteers. Such an approach will probably help, but for many pastors such tactics feel artificial. The long-term effect of such an approach is that the congregation will see the pastor's leadership as disconnected from preaching. This is a grave mistake, because preaching is our primary leadership platform.

Another common solution is to preach a special sermon for every ministry each year: a missions sermon, a small group sermon, an evangelism sermon, and so forth. We are naïve if we think one sermon a year will keep people fired up about a particular ministry. And as a church grows, the number of these sermons multiplies.

## The answer: regular application

A better solution is to include ministry departments in our sermon application process. We may think of application as occurring "out there" in a member's life with family, career, friendships, and community, and fail to think through the relevance of a biblical text for our church environment. Instead, keep a list of church ministries handy as you prepare sermon application. Ask yourself, "What does a response to this particular biblical text look like in children's ministry? Student ministry? Missions? Small groups?"

For example, in a series through 1 and 2 Timothy, which was not designed to meet the needs of any particular ministry, I was able to promote church ministries in roughly two-thirds of the sermons.

In a sermon on 1 Timothy 1:12–20, I promoted our children's ministry. The sermon's main idea was "the good news of Jesus Christ is able to transform all kinds of people." In reference to verses 18–19, I emphasized, "The good news of Jesus Christ is able to transform people raised in godly homes." In describing Timothy's early life, I talked about people who like Timothy were raised in a godly home, which provided a natural segue into our children's ministry.

I said, "Every Christian parent wants their son or daughter to be a Timothy. This is why it's important for our children's ministry to partner with us in nurturing our kids in the faith. That's why we won't put just anyone in our children's ministry. It's not babysitting. This quarter we're short a few volunteers. If you're interested in helping the kids of this church become like Timothy, let us know. We'll provide the training if you have a willing heart."

In a sermon based on 2 Timothy 3:10–17, I was able to promote a major change in our church's youth ministry. Our youth pastor felt we needed to better integrate our students with the rest of our congregation, so we decided to eliminate our Sunday morning meeting time for students and encourage our youth to attend worship services with their parents or friends. I preached this sermon a few months prior to this change. One of my subpoints was "prepared Christians seek godly mentors." This provided a natural opportunity to talk about the impending change.

"Those of us with students know that in the fall our student ministry is going to move its Sunday morning youth service to Saturday nights. When that change occurs, we will encourage our junior high and senior high students to attend worship services with their parents. One driving reason for this change is to help our students build stronger relationships with adults.

Our youth pastor wants to help students find godly mentors in their lives, and he knows that worshiping together can help build these kinds of relationships."

I was able to voice public support of our youth pastor's change as well as anticipate some of the resistance by addressing the purpose of the change.

Finally, in a sermon on 2 Timothy 4:1–8, I promoted our small group ministry. My sermon title was "The Church God Uses," and one of my subpoints was "God uses churches that are committed to communicating the Bible" (v. 2). Here I spoke about the need not just to hear about the Bible, but actually to apply it and live it. I said, "This is why we offer small groups, so people can gather together and learn to apply the Bible to their lives." I followed this with a story about a person in our church who learned to apply a biblical principle in his small group. Then I invited people to get into a group and gave them a way to respond.

> *When I use sermon application to promote ministries, I feel confident and passionate.*

## Benefits

I find this approach helpful because it is proactive. Rather than waiting for church leaders to come to me, I am able to promote their ministries regularly without request. This builds trust. They might say, "We could use a shot in the arm if it fits with your sermon this month," but no longer do they come out of desperation.

This approach also roots my leadership in the Scriptures. When I promote ministries without a scriptural basis, I feel like a salesperson. I'm not a good salesperson, and I don't like the feeling of having to "peddle" the church's ministry. But when I use sermon application to promote ministries, I feel confident and passionate. If involvement in that ministry is a legitimate application of the biblical text, I can speak with authority.

Finally, by connecting ministry promotion to my sermons, I model commitment to the authority of Scripture. People see that I don't challenge people to do whatever I want them to do. As a leader, I live under the authority of Scripture.

**Timothy J. Peck** is director of the chapel and a lecturer in the school of theology at Azusa Pacific University, Azusa, California. He preaches regularly at Christ Our King Church in Azusa.

# NOTES

## Notes to Chapter 1: As One Approved

1. Here are two good definitions of expository preaching: "Expository preaching is the communication of a biblical concept, derived from and transmitted through a historical, grammatical, and literary study of a passage in its context, which the Holy Spirit first applies to the personality and experience of the preacher, then through him to his hearers." Haddon W. Robinson, *Expository Preaching* (Leicester, UK: InterVarsity, 1986), 20. "Expository preaching is 'Bible-centered preaching.' That is, it is handling the text 'in such a way that its real and essential meaning as it existed in the mind of the particular Biblical writer and as it exists in the light of the over-all context of Scripture is made plain and applied to the present-day needs of the hearers.'" Sidney Greidanus, *The Modern Preacher and the Ancient Text* (Grand Rapids: Eerdmans, 1988), 11, quoting Merrill Unger, *Principles of Expository Preaching* (Grand Rapids: Zondervan, 1955), 33. Cf. Richard L. Mayhue, "Rediscovering Expository Preaching," *The Master's Seminary Journal* 1 (1990): 119.

2. Frederick Dale Bruner and William Hordern, *The Holy Spirit: The Shy Member of the Trinity* (1983; repr. Eugene, OR: Wipf & Stock, 2001), 24–25.

3. Ibid., 26.

4. Ibid., 30–31.

5. Ibid., 21–22.

6. What the church today needs is a theology of the redemption of time. E.g., Jonathan Edwards's sermon "The Preciousness of Time, and the Importance of Redeeming It," in *The Works of Jonathan Edwards,* ed. Edward Hickman, 2 vols. (repr., Carlisle, PA: Banner of Truth, 1992), 2:233–236. Two samples from Edwards of such theology should suffice: "Time is so short, and the work which we have to do in it is so great, that we have none of it to spare" (2:233–234). "There is nothing more precious, and yet nothing of which men are more prodigal" (2:234). Perhaps also a rabbinic theology of study is needed: "The world endures because of three activities: study of Torah, worship, and deeds of lovingkindness" (Mishnah, *Avot* 1:2); "These are the activities whose benefit a man can enjoy in this world but whose principle remains undiminished for him in the world to come: honoring father and mother, deeds of lovingkindness, making peace between a man and his fellow. The study of Torah, however, equals all of these put together" (Mishnah, *Peah* 1:1). Cf. Mishnah, *Peah* 1:1; Babylonian Talmud, *Menahot* 110a; Babylonian Talmud, *Sanhedrin* 59a. I am grateful to Dr. Michael Graves for these rabbinic references.

7. For a grander overview of this theme, see T. David Gordon, *Why Johnny Can't Preach: The Media Have Shaped the Messengers* (Phillipsburg, PA: P&R, 2009).

8. For further study on hermeneutics, my favorite book on the subject is Dan McCartney and Charles Clayton, *Let the Reader Understand: A Guide to Interpreting and Applying the Bible,* 2nd ed. (Phillipsburg, PA: P&R, 2002). Cf. Gordon D. Fee and Douglas Stuart, *How to Read the Bible for All Its Worth,* 3rd ed. (Grand Rapids: Zondervan, 2003), and Graeme Goldsworthy, *Gospel-Centered Hermeneutics: Foundations and Principles of Evangelical Biblical Interpretation* (Downers Grove, IL: InterVarsity, 2010).

9. See Dick Lucas, "Preaching the Melodic Line," chap. 3 in this volume.

10. What Murray J. Harris said of recent commentaries on the Gospel of John ("what an embarrassment of riches we now have!") is true of many books of the Bible. See his book review of J. Ramsey Michaels, *The Gospel of John,* New International Commentary on the New Testament, in *Themelios* 36, no. 1 (April 2011): 102–103.

11. As noted and translated by John Piper, in John Piper and D. A. Carson, *The Pastor as Scholar and the Scholar as Pastor: Reflections on Life and Ministry* (Wheaton, IL: Crossway, 2011), 28.

## Notes to Chapter 6: Soul Sermons from Psalms

1. Dan B. Allender and Tremper Longman III, *The Cry of the Soul: How Our Emotions Reveal Our Deepest Questions about God* (Colorado Springs: NavPress, 1994), 31.

2. Tremper Longman III, *Reading the Bible with Heart and Mind* (Colorado Springs: NavPress, 1997), 131.

3. Thomas G. Long, *Preaching and the Literary Forms of the Bible* (Philadelphia: Fortress, 1989), 24–34.

4. Craig Loscalzo, "A Rhetorical Model," in *Hermeneutics for Preaching: Approaches to Contemporary Interpretations of Scripture*, ed. Raymond Bailey (Nashville: Broadman, 1992), 105.

5. Long, *Preaching and the Literary Forms,* 24–34.

6. For a helpful discussion on establishing a point of view in sermons, see David Buttrick, *Homiletic: Moves and Structures* (Philadelphia: Fortress, 1987), 55–68.

7. W. H. Bellinger, *Psalms: Reading and Studying the Book of Praises* (Peabody, MA: Hendrickson, 1990), 36.

8. Long, *Preaching and the Literary Forms,* 24–34.

9. Bellinger, *Psalms,* 36.

10. Carl Sagan, quoted in Donald Williams, *Psalms 1–72* (vol. 13 of Mastering the Old Testament: A Book-by-Book Commentary by Today's Great Bible Teachers; ed. Lloyd J. Ogilvie; Dallas: Word, 1986), 74.

11. Martin Rees, *Just Six Numbers: The Deep Forces That Shape the Universe* (New York: Basic Books, 2000), 10.

12. Alter, Robert. *The Art of Biblical Poetry* (New York: Basic Books, 1985).

Greidanus, Sidney. *The Modern Preacher and the Ancient Text: Interpreting and Preaching Biblical Literature* (Grand Rapids: Eerdmans, 1988).

Kaiser, Walter C., Jr. *Toward an Exegetical Theology: Biblical Exegesis for Preaching and Teaching* (Grand Rapids: Baker, 1996).

Kaiser, Walter C., Jr., and Moisés Silva. *An Introduction to Biblical Hermeneutics: The Search for Meaning* (Grand Rapids: Zondervan, 1994).

Klein, William W., Craig L. Blomberg, and Robert L. Hubbard, Jr. *Introduction to Biblical Interpretation*, ed. Kermit A. Ecklebarger (Dallas: Word, 1993).

Kugel, James L. *The Idea of Biblical Poetry: Parallelism and Its History* (1981; repr., Ann Arbor, MI: UMI Books on Demand, 1997).

Longman, Tremper III. *How to Read the Psalms* (Downers Grove, IL: InterVarsity, 1988).

Schaefer, Konrad. "Psalms," *Berit Olam: Studies in Hebrew Narrative and Poetry*, ed. David W. Cotter, Jerome T. Walsh, and Chris Franke (Collegeville, MN: Liturgical Press, 2001).

## Notes to Chapter 7: The Fundamentals of Sermon Application (part 1)

1. David Larsen, *The Anatomy of Preaching: Identifying the Issues in Preaching Today* (Grand Rapids: Kregel, 1989).

2. Lori Carrell, *The Great American Sermon Survey* (Wheaton, IL: Mainstay, 2000), 88, 113–114.

3. Quoted in John A. Broadus, *A Treatise on the Preparation and Delivery of Sermons* (Nashville: Barbee and Smith, 1894), 230.

4. William Perkins, *The Art of Prophesying* (1592; repr., Carlisle, PA: Banner of Truth), 54. Paul Koptak's definition is also good: "Application is the process by which preachers demonstrate the contemporary significance of a biblical teaching in a particular context. Put more directly, application grows out of the preacher's desire to speak words that will be used by the Holy Spirit to bring about changes in the lives of believers and believing communities." *The New Interpreter's Handbook of Preaching,* s.v. "application" (Nashville: Abingdon, 2008), 176.

5. Ian Pitt-Watson, *Preaching: A Kind of Folly* (Philadelphia: Westminster, 1976), 58.

6. Randal Pelton, "Preaching for True Holiness," in *The Art and Craft of Biblical Preaching,* ed. Haddon Robinson and Craig Brian Larson (Grand Rapids: Zondervan, 2004), 311.

7. Table 7.1 expands the ideas of Haddon Robinson (*Biblical Preaching*) and Donald Sunukjian (*Invitation to Biblical Preaching*, 87–127).

8. One of those authors is Old Testament scholar Walter Kaiser, following the theories of E. D. Hirsch (*Validity in Interpretation*). See Kaiser, *Toward an Exegetical Theology: Biblical Exegesis for Preaching and Teaching* (Grand Rapids: Baker, 1981), 31–33.

9. See Mark Allan Powell, *What Do They Hear?* (Nashville: Abingdon, 2007).

10. See Jay E. Adams, *Preaching with Purpose: The Urgent Task of Homiletics* (Grand Rapids: Zondervan, 1982), 131–137.

11. Bernard Ramm, *Protestant Biblical Interpretation*, 3rd ed. (Grand Rapids: Baker, 1985), 113. Similarly, Old Testament scholar John Sailhammer says, "A text is . . . an embodiment of an author's intention, that is, a strategy designed to carry out that intention." *Introduction to Old Testament Theology* (Grand Rapids: Baker, 1995), 46–47.

12. Jay Adams states, "In bridging the gap, avoid the endless discussions of 'meaning' and 'significance.' Instead, look for the original intent, the *telos* of the passage." *Truth Applied: Application in Preaching* (Grand Rapids: Zondervan, 1990), 49.

13. Daniel Overdorf, *Applying the Sermon* (Grand Rapids: Kregel, 2009), 80.

## Notes to Chapter 8: The Fundamentals of Sermon Application (part 2)

1. Haddon Robinson, *Biblical Preaching,* 2nd ed. (Grand Rapids: Baker, 2002), 108.

2. To learn how to exegete *telos*, see Jay E. Adams, *Truth Applied: Application in Preaching* (Grand Rapids: Zondervan, 1990), and *Preaching with Purpose: The Urgent Task of Homiletics* (Grand Rapids: Zondervan, 1982). Also helpful are Gordon Fee and Douglas Stuart, *How to Read the Bible for All Its Worth*, 3rd ed. (Grand Rapids: Zondervan, 1993), and Walter Kaiser, *Toward an Exegetical Theology* (Grand Rapids: Baker Academic, 1998).

3. Bryan Chapell, *Christ-Centered Preaching: Redeeming the Expository Sermon,* 2nd ed. (Grand Rapids: Baker, 1994). Other homileticians have similar concepts, such as Haddon Robinson's "human factor" (*Biblical Preaching*) and Paul Scott Wilson's "trouble" (*Four Pages of the Sermon*).

4. Adams, *Truth Applied*, 48. Adams uses the same example in *Preaching with Purpose.*

5. Timothy Keller, "Preaching Amid Pluralism," in *The Art and Craft of Biblical Preaching,* ed. Haddon Robinson and Craig Brian Larson (Grand Rapids: Zondervan, 2004), 178.

6. Fred Craddock, *Preaching* (Nashville: Abingdon, 1985), 95–98.

7. Chapell, *Christ-Centered Preaching*, 206.

8. Quoted in Adams, *Truth Applied*, 80–81.

9. Haddon Robinson, "Blending Bible Content with Life Application," in *Art and Craft*, 299.

10. Adams, Jay E. *Preaching with Purpose: The Urgent Task of Homiletics* (Grand Rapids: Zondervan, 1982).

Adams, Jay E. *Truth Applied: Application in Preaching* (Grand Rapids: Zondervan, 1990).

Chapell, Bryan. *Christ-Centered Preaching: Redeeming the Expository Sermon* 2nd ed. (Grand Rapids: Baker, 1994).

Overdorf, Daniel. *Applying the Sermon* (Grand Rapids: Kregel, 2009).

Robinson, Haddon. *Biblical Preaching: The Development and Delivery of Expository Messages*, 2nd ed. (Grand Rapids: Baker, 2002).

Sunukjian, Donald R. *Invitation to Biblical Preaching: Proclaiming Truth with Clarity and Relevance* (Grand Rapids: Kregel, 2007).

## Note to Chapter 9: Blending Bible Content and Life Application

1. This chapter is taken from the book *Mastering Contemporary Preaching*; copyright © 1989 by Christianity Today, Inc.